Super Cool
JOKES
& GAMES
For Kids!

Bob Phillips

HARVEST HOUSE™ PUBLISHERS

EUGENE, OREGON

All Scripture references in this book are taken from the King James Version of the Bible.

Cover by Terry Dugan Design, Minneapolis, Minnesota.

Illustrated by Norm Daniels.

SUPER COOL JOKES AND GAMES FOR KIDS
(formerly titled Silly Stunts and Terrific Tricks)
Copyright © 1997 by Harvest House Publishers
Eugene, Oregon 97402

ISBN 0-7369-0754-8

Printed in the United States of America.

03 04 05 06 07 08 09 10 / BC / 10 9 8 7 6 5 4

Super Cool
JOKES
& GAMES
For Kids!

Contents

Fresh from the Funny Farm
Brain-Benders 13
A Square Deal 20
Humorous Bible Riddles #1 21

Party Fun
    This Is My Knee 22
    The Bionic Brain 23
    The Baffling Box 24
The Vanishing Vase 26
Word Puzzles #1 27
Crazy Pictures #1 28

Totally Tricky
    You Can't Be Wrong 29
    Super String 30
    Straight Arrow 30
    Beans 31
    Old MacDonald 31
    A Touchy Problem 32
Baffling Blocks 33
Humorous Bible Riddles #2 34

Practical Jokes
    Two Dots 36
    Emergency 36
    Typewriter 37
    The Big Push 37
    Crazy Person 38
    Nose Drop 38
    The Last Straw 39
    Potfor 39

Updock 40
Warning.................................... 40
Did You Hear?. 41
Crazy Stairs 42
Word Puzzles #2 43
Crazy Pictures #2 44
Match This #1 45
Triangle Trouble 46

Flim-Flam
The Exact Word 47
The Magic Hat 47
A Good Turn............................... 48
Strong As a Rope 48
An Impossible Task......................... 49
Top This................................... 50
Add by Subtracting 50
Double Twister............................. 51
Ten Thousand.............................. 51
The Shrinking Quarter 52
Double the Hoop 53
Humorous Bible Riddles #3 55

Crazy Stunts
Jumping Jehoshaphat 56
The Vanishing Sugar Packet.................. 57
Full of Air 58
Following Orders........................... 58
Sticky Fingers.............................. 59
The Triangle Box................................ 60
Humorous Bible Riddles #4 61

Pick These
The Lumberjack............................ 62
Old MacDonald's Corral 63
Six to Three................................ 64
The Builder's Challenge 64

Three to Four 65
The Big Question 66
Thought Twisters 67
Banana 70
Word Puzzles #3 71

Fantastic Card Tricks
    The Ace of Spades 72
    Follow the Leader 73
    Eyes in the Back of Your Head. 75
    Marvelous Magic 76
    Same 'O / Same 'O 77
    Fingerprints 78
    Lie Detector Test. 79
    Traveling to the Bottom. 81
    Flying Card Fun. 83
    Bamboozled 83
    Mr. Know-It-All 84
The Builder's Nightmare. 87
Humorous Bible Riddles #5 88

Party Tricks
    Let's Go for a Spin 90
    Spock's Brain Transfer. 91
    A Hole in One. 92
Up or Down. 94

Tricky Fun
    X-Ray Vision 95
    Spoon Hanging 95
    Magic Knife. 96
    Imaginary Glue 97
    I Know the Answer 98
    Turn Over in the Grave 98
    Floating Metal 98
    The Rule of the Game 99
    Autographed Fruit. 99

The Magic Moving Box 101
Humorous Bible Riddles #6 102
The Eye Twister. 103

Pranks
    Too Many T's 104
    Refrigerator. 104
    Television 105
    Owah. 105
    Frozen Water. 105
    Flip-Flop Word 105
    A Sticky Problem 106
    Slap on the Back. 106
    Rembrandt 106
    The Power of Ten. 107
    Button, Button, Who's Got the Button? 107
    Ten Thousand. 107
    Rattlesnake Eggs 108
Triangle Time. 110
Word Puzzles #4 111

Wild Stunts
    Easy Money. 112
    Breakout 112
    Creep Around the Chair 113
    The Karate Straw 113
Parallel Puzzle. 115
Humorous Bible Riddles #7 116

More Flim-Flam
    Super Brain. 117
    The Frightened Finger. 117
    Quick Hands. 118
    Going Bananas 118
    Blowhard. 119
    Air Force 120
    Very Impressive 120

Handcuffed................................... 121
Math Wizard............................... 122
Word Puzzles #5 123
Crazy Pictures #3 124
Mind Warpers................................. 125
Tantalizing Triangle 129
Match This #2 130
Crazy Pictures #4 131
Humorous Bible Riddles #8 132
Math Magic.................................... 134

Answer Key.................................... 137

Fresh from the Funny Farm

Welcome to the wild and wacky world of whimsical wit! You're embarking on a joyful journey of jolly jokes and jests. Soon you will captivate the interest of your friends, charm strangers, and confuse your family. You will be an expert in performing pranks, pulling practical jokes, and presenting puzzling illusions.

Flamboyant fun and fanciful frolic will fill the air when you do fantastic card tricks. Your frazzled friends will be flabbergasted with your funny flim-flams. Your funky fun will give you flash and flair and make you famous!

Kids will drive their parents to the nuthouse. Parents will bamboozle their children. Aunts and uncles will confuse their nieces and nephews. Grandparents will baffle their grandchildren. Teachers will get even with students. And youth directors will pull practical jokes on teens.

Yes, you'll brilliantly beguile your pals with the "Brain Benders." You'll be the talk of the town when you tease your friends with the "Totally Tricky Tricks." You'll be an expert in verbal hocus-pocus. This book is better than laughing gas—or a poke in the eye with a sharp stick.

After my last book, they locked me up for another 11 years. But I fooled them. I paid one of the orderlies $17,369 to sneak out my new manuscript. (He told me I was getting a good deal, and it made sense to me.) George Washington, who lives next door, and my friend Napoleon from across the hall thought my last book was brilliant. They encouraged me to scribble out a new one.

Because of my strong desire to become an expert in classical writing technique and intense brain pressure, you now have *Super Cool Jokes & Games for Kids!*

I know this book will increase your wisdom and make you smart like I am . . . I am . . . I am. I've got to stop writing now. I hear the steps of the little men in white coats. They are bringing me my favorite white jacket. You know, the one with all the straps on it.

—Bob Phillips
From the Fresno Funny Farm

Brain-Benders

🌀

1. Katherine had just been given an engagement ring with a big diamond in it. But when she was in the kitchen getting breakfast ready, she had an accident. Her ring was a little loose and it slipped off her finger and fell smack into some coffee. But the diamond didn't get wet. How was this possible?

2. Kirk went to a pet store to purchase a beautiful parrot. The owner of the store said, "I guarantee that this beautiful parrot will repeat every word it hears." Kirk took the parrot home and started talking to it. The parrot didn't repeat a single word that was spoken to it. Yet, what the salesman said about the bird was true. How could this be?

3. Nole was riding his bicycle home from soccer practice when he saw a group of men. They were talking about a large truck that was in the road by the underpass. He rode over to them and listened to their

discussion. He learned that the truck was one inch too tall to squeeze beneath the underpass. The men were trying to figure out what to do. Nole looked down the street and saw a service station. He turned to the men and said, "I think I know how to solve your problem." What do you think Nole's bright idea was?

4. What is the secret of keeping a moron in suspense?

5. There once was a race horse
   That won great fame.
   What-do-you-think
   Was the horse's name.

6. Mr. Anderson had a very old house that was built in the form of a square. At each corner of his house there was a large boulder. He wanted to tear down his old house and build a new one that was double the size of his old house. He wanted to keep the new house in the form of a square and still use the same location, but he could not move the boulders. How did Mr. Anderson solve the problem?

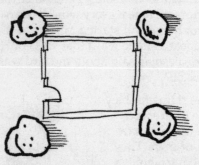

7. A big game hunter was walking through the jungle when he became lost. After awhile he ran across a native. The hunter said to the native, "Am I heading in the right direction to get to the water hole where the

zebras drink?" The native stuck her finger in her ear. The hunter realized that the native could understand him but was unable to communicate very well. The hunter didn't know if sticking a finger in an ear meant yes or no. By asking one more question, he was able to find out the answer. What was his second question?

8. Would it be possible to hang a hat over a projection, blindfold a man, hand him a rifle, lead him 100 yards away, have him point the rifle toward the hat, pull the trigger—and have the man successfully hit the hat while his blindfold was still in place? If your answer is yes, how would it be possible?

9. What very strange seven-letter word has three "U's" in it?

10. When you look at a mirror, it appears as if your right hand is on the left, and your left hand is on the right. Yet, the top is not the bottom, and the bottom is not the top. Why is this?

11. Everyone knows that the month of February is the shortest month in the year. It has 28 days (29 in a leap year). However, very few people know what the second shortest month of the year is. Do you have any idea?

12. One day a great explorer decided to visit the North Pole. He started in the United States. He knew that the points to the compass were:

N
W E
S

North was above him, south was behind him, west was on his left, and east was on his right. When the explorer reached the North Pole, he kept on walking for a mile. South was now above him, north was behind him, west was now on his right side, and east was on his left side. What is wrong with this statement?

13. Somewhere on this page is a word that is mispelled. Can you find it?

14. There is a secret Christmas message in the letters below. See if you can find it.

ABCDEFGHIJKMNOPQRSTUVWXYZ

15. Mr. and Mrs. Lilley had nine sons. They each had a sister. How many children did the Lilleys have?

16. A horse can grow to be 16 or 17 hands high. Each hand equals 4 inches. Some horses can be as wide as 3 feet. How many large horses can you put into an empty barn that measures 70 feet long by 40 feet wide?

17. Mr. Hilts had a box to hold tennis balls. On the floor around him, there were 47 tennis balls. As Mr. Hilts picked up the tennis balls and put them in the box, the number of tennis balls in his box doubled every 20 seconds. At 3:00 P.M., his box was full. What time was it when his box was half full?

18. Can you solve the following math problem? Which of the following signs should be placed inside the brackets: +/−/×?

$$5 [\ ] 5 [\ ] 5 [\ ] 5 = 100$$

19. Albert Einstein was once asked, "What do you take off last before you get into bed?" What was Mr. Einstein's answer?

20. Sherlock Holmes was called to solve a difficult mystery. At the location of the mystery, he found Willard and Elmo lying dead on the floor. He looked around for clues and found a broken glass bowl. He could find no marks on Willard and Elmo. He looked for signs of poisoning, but he could not find any. How did he solve the mystery?

21. In the 1880s, all cowboys loved to shoot their pistols. Some cowboys became outlaws. Some of the outlaw cowboys shot and killed people. Which of the following statements is correct?

    A. All cowboys in the 1880s were outlaws.

    B. All cowboys in the 1880s were killers.

    C. Some cowboys enjoyed shooting their pistols.

    D. All outlaw cowboys were killers.

22. A night watchman was assigned to guard the vault at a bank in a small midwest town. The bank was filled with gold bars and the payroll for the only factory in

town. In the morning, the night watchman went to the bank president with the following story:

> Last night I dreamed that a group of robbers were going to holdup the bank and steal the gold bars and payroll. They were planning to come this next Sunday while everyone was in church.

The bank president was alarmed. On Saturday night, he planted extra guards in the bank. Sure enough, the next morning robbers attempted to steal the gold and payroll. The extra guards caught them and put them in jail.

The next Monday, the watchman was fired. Why did the bank president fire him?

23. Mr. Williams owned an orange ranch. He was in the habit of planting the orange trees in a straight line at intervals of 20 feet between the trees. In one row he planted 20 orange trees. What was the distance between the two end trees in that row?

24. How many letters are there in the Egyptian alphabet? Here are two clues: The Egyptian alphabet has the same amount of letters as the Algerian alphabet, but it has one less than the Mongolian alphabet.

25. If you had two rattlesnakes in front of a rattlesnake, and two rattlesnakes behind a rattlesnake, and one rattlesnake in the middle, how many rattlesnakes would you have?

26. Some hockey players are amateurs. All amateurs play without financial reward—many with great enthusiasm. Which of the following statements is true?

   A. Hockey players all play without financial reward.
   B. All amateurs are enthusiastic hockey players.
   C. Some hockey players play with great enthusiasm.

27. There was a terrible forest fire. A ranger called for airplanes to drop water on the raging inferno. One pilot loaded water in his plane and flew over the fire. He tried to open the release doors for the water to come out and drop on the fire. He pushed the button, but the water did not come out. Why not?

28. Sherlock Holmes went out to solve a great mystery. At the location, he found seven pieces of coal, a scarf with a knot in it, and a beat-up old hat. All of these items were lying on a green lawn that had not been mowed. He looked around for other clues but did not find any. What was the mystery on the lawn?

A Square Deal

How many squares are in the puzzle below?

Humorous Bible Riddles #1

1. Certain days in the Bible passed by more quickly than most. Which days were these?

2. Matthew and Mark have something that is not found in Luke and John. What is it?

3. Which one of Noah's sons was considered a clown?

4. What was the first game played in the Bible?

5. What made Abraham so smart?

6. What is usually black, sometimes brown or white, but should be red?

7. Why did everyone on the ark think that the horses were pessimistic?

8. Who was the first person in the Bible to have surgery performed on him?

9. When was the Red Sea very angry?

10. What vegetable did Noah not want on the ark?

Party Fun

This Is My Knee

This is a good party-starter game. The leader informs the group that they should say and do the opposite of what he does.

For example, the leader will point to his head and say, "This is my knee." The group then responds by pointing at their knees and saying, "This is my head." To put the pressure on, the leader will count to five after he points to a body part. The group has to the count of five to do just the opposite. The trick is that everyone will not be able to do the opposite.

It is good to have about 10 different body parts and places to point to. Be sure to quit while the group is still having fun.

The Bionic Brain

Hand out pieces of paper and pencils to your group. Have them write a word or short phrase on their pieces of paper, then fold them up. Have a person from the group pick up the folded pieces of paper and hand them to you.

Tell the group that you will demonstrate your "bionic brain." Explain that your brain has the power to absorb the messages written on the pieces of paper without looking at what is written.

Next, hold one of the folded pieces of paper to your forehead. Pull it down, still unfolded, and say, "Did someone in the group write (whatever the word or short phrase might be). A person will say, "Yes, I did." Open the paper and see if that is correct.

Proceed to do the same thing, holding folded slips to your forehead, and telling what word or phrase is written on it. Continue to do this until you have a perfect score. Your friends will be amazed.

With this trick, you need a secret helper in the group. Agree ahead of time what word or phrase your helper will write. After everyone has finished writing his word or phrase, have your secret helper collect all the folded pieces of paper. Your helper will be sure that his piece of paper (with the agreed upon word or phrase) will be on the bottom of the stack.

When you pick up the top piece of paper and put it to your forehead, quote your secret helper's word or phrase (not the one on the paper). He will immediately respond by saying, "I wrote that"—even though that is not what is really written on the paper you're holding.

When you open up the first piece of paper you will see the next word or phrase that you will want to quote. Say to the group, "That's correct, that is what [your secret helper] wrote."

Hold up the second piece of paper to your forehead, and quote what was written on the first piece of paper. Continue to do this until all the pieces of paper have been read. Your friends will never guess how you did the trick. Don't tell them.

Be sure that after looking at the next word or phrase you place it upside down in your lap or on something. You don't want someone near you to see that what you're quoting is not written on the piece of paper.

Practice the trick before you demonstrate it in public. Take six pieces of paper and write a different name or phrase on each piece. Circle one of the names or phrases and put it on the bottom of the stack. Work through this practice stack several times until you get comfortable reading one thing and quoting another.

The Baffling Box

At a party, tell your friends that you have the ability to send messages to your assistant by using your mind and the "baffling box."

Draw an imaginary box on the ground and an imaginary cross in the middle of it. Ask your assistant to leave the room. Then point to one of your friends and say, "You are selected." Call your assistant back into the room and stand in the imaginary baffling box. Ask your assistant to point out who was selected. To the amazement of everyone, your assistant will pick out the selected person.

The trick is very simple. When you draw the baffling box on the ground, pause for a moment. Both you and your assistant have previously agreed that the first person to speak after you draw the box will be the person you will select.

Have your assistant leave the room. Point to the individual that first spoke after you drew the baffling box. Tell him that he is the selected person. Have your assistant come back into the room. He or she will identify the right individual. You can do this trick several times and no one will catch on. Don't worry about whether someone will speak after you draw the baffling box. Someone will talk.

The Vanishing Vase

Look carefully at the picture of the vase. Can you see the two men who are facing each other? When you see the two men the vase vanishes. When you focus on the white vase the two men disappear. Once you see both the vase and the men you will have a hard time focusing on either one of them.

Word Puzzles #1

See if you can identify these word puzzles.

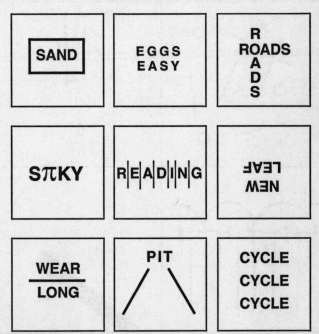

Crazy Pictures #1

See if you can identify the pictures below . . .

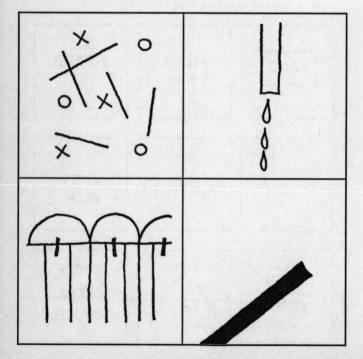

Totally Tricky

You Can't Be Wrong

This is a trick that you can use time and time again. You will need three coins that are the same (three pennies, dimes, nickels, or quarters).

Pull the three quarters out of your pocket and place them on a counter or table in front of you. Turn to your friend and ask, "Do you see these four quarters?" He will say, "No, I see three quarters."

You respond by saying, "No, four quarters." As soon as you say that, you begin counting the quarters pointing in their general direction but not touching them: "One, two, three, four."

Your friend will still say, "Three quarters."

You repeat, "No, four quarters." Then count them again as you did before. Then say, "I see four quarters and you see three quarters, is that correct?"

"Yes, that's correct."

"No," you respond, "there are four quarters." Then count them again as before. Then say, "You see three quarters, and I see four. If I'm wrong, will you buy me a Coke?" Then quickly count the coins one more time.

Your friend will think he's got you and will say OK. Then you say, "I'm wrong. Where's my Coke?"

Super String

For this trick you need a full glass of water with an ice cube floating in it and a piece of string. You will also need salt in a salt shaker (placed inconspicuously nearby).

Tell your friend that you have a piece of "Super String." Say, "With this piece of string I will be able to lift the ice cube out of the glass of water."

Hand the string to your friend and say, "Here, you try it." After he tries it for a little while, he will give up.

Ask your friend if he thinks you can lift the ice cube out of the water with the super string. The answer will probably be no. "I'll bet I can," you reply.

Take the string and carefully lay one end across the ice cube. Then take some salt and sprinkle it along the string. The salt will melt the ice slightly. Wait a few seconds for the ice to reform around the string, then slowly lift the ice cube from the glass.

This can also be done with a hair from your head. It is even more impressive when you lift an ice cube with "Super Hair."

Straight Arrow

Take a piece of strong paper (like a 3 × 5 card) and draw an arrow on it. Place the card on a table, leaning it against some object with the arrow pointing to the right.

Tell your friend to look carefully at the arrow. Say, "I'll bet you that I can make that arrow turn to the left without touching the card or moving the table in any way."

Your friend will probably study the arrow for a little while and say, "Prove it. I'll bet you can't do it."

Just smile and say, "I'll bet I can." Then grab a full glass of water and place it in front of the arrow. Have your friend look at the arrow through the glass of water. The arrow will point left!

Beans

You will need two pieces of paper, a pencil, and some beans for this trick.

Draw a large circle on one piece of paper and put the beans inside of it.

Challenge your friend to sit down at a table and take beans out of the circle with one hand while writing his name and address on the other sheet of paper with his other hand. Both hands should be moving at the same time.

He will not be able to do it.

Old MacDonald

Turn to your friends and say, "I'll bet I can sing the 'Old MacDonald Had a Farm' song backward."

They will probably say, "Let's see you do it."

Simply turn around with your back to your friends and sing the song.

A Touchy Problem

Turn to your friend and say, "I'll bet you can't stick out your tongue and touch your nose." Your friend will try, but he will fail.

Now say, "I'll bet I can stick out my tongue and touch my nose."

Your friend will probably say, "No way!"

You say, "I'll show you how." With that, stick out your tongue and touch your nose with your finger.

Baffling Blocks

As you study the drawing of the blocks, are you looking down at the blocks, or are you looking up at the blocks?

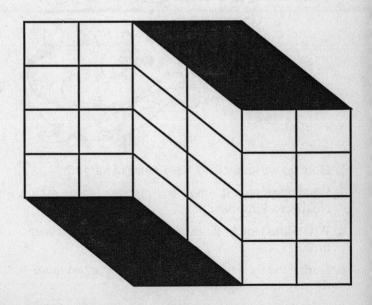

Humorous Bible Riddles #2

1. Why do you think Jonah couldn't trust the ocean?

2. How do we know God has a sense of humor?

3. What time was it when the hippopotamus sat on Noah's rocking chair?

4. What does God both give away and keep at the same time?

5. During the six days of creation, which weighed more—the day or the night?

6. What did the skunks on the ark have that no other animals had?

7. What type of tea does the Bible suggest we not drink?

8. In what book of the Bible do we find something that is in modern-day courtrooms?

9. Which animal on the ark was the rudest?

10. What kind of soap does God use to keep the oceans clean?

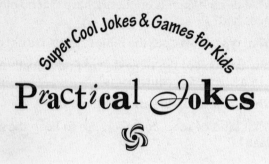

Practical Jokes

Two Dots

Gently turn the palm of your friend's hand upward. Then take a ball-point pen and make two small dots in the palm of your friend's hand. While you are holding his hand with your left hand, look at him and say, "Do you know the difference between those two dots on your hand?"

He will probably say no.

Then take your pen and begin to point at one of the dots. Say, "This one (touching one of the dots with the point of the pen) has a long tail on it." Quickly draw a long line with the pen before he can move his hand. You will have gotten your friend with this practical joke. Don't worry about the ink on his hand. It will wash off.

Emergency

Take a piece of paper and fold it over. On the outside write the following:

IN CASE OF EMERGENCY
OPEN THIS PAPER

On the inside of the paper write:

NOT NOW, SILLY—
IN CASE OF EMERGENCY!

Leave the piece of paper around for one of your friends to discover.

Typewriter

Ask your friend if she has ever played typewriter. She will probably say no.

Have your friend hold both of her arms straight out in front of her. Ask her to fold her arms, one arm over the other, holding her elbows about shoulder height.

Tell your friend that the folded arms are where the typewriter keys are located. Put your hands on her folded arms and pretend to type. Tell your friend that when typists came to the end of a sentence on older typewriters they had to grab the arm bar and shift the paper upward and a bell would ring.

As you are typing with your fingers *and* telling the story at the same time, quickly reach out with your left hand like you are going to grab the shift lever. Bring your hand back and (lightly) tap the right cheek of your friend's face. As your hand touches her face make a "ding" sound like the ringing of the typewriter bell. Get ready to run!

The Big Push

Take a piece of paper and cut a hole in it. Make the hole about the size of a quarter.

Tell your friend, "I'll bet that I can push you through this hole in the paper."

Your friend will probably say, "I'll bet you can't."

Take the piece of paper and hold it up to his body. Then take your finger, put it through the hole, and push him.

Crazy Person

Take a piece of paper and on one side write the following:

HOW TO KEEP A CRAZY PERSON
BUSY ALL DAY.

PLEASE TURN THIS OVER.

On the back side of the paper write the following:

HOW TO KEEP A CRAZY PERSON
BUSY ALL DAY.

PLEASE TURN THIS OVER.

Nose Drop

You will get a lot of laughs with this one.

Ask your friend if she has ever played nose drop. Of course she will say no.

Then explain, "You take a quarter and, starting just above the bridge of your nose, see if you can roll it off the tip of your nose. It looks easy, but it's not." Show her how to do it a few times. (Loosely holding the coin between her thumb and forefinger, she rolls the coin on its edge.) Let her try it several times.

Then say, "Are you ready to play?" Grab a piece of paper, a pencil, and your quarter. Put the quarter on the paper and trace a circle around the quarter three times. Make six of these circles on the paper. Make sure your pencil touches the quarter.

Next, place the paper on the floor in front of your friend. Tell her to try rolling it off her nose again, only this time attempt to make the quarter land on the paper. If the quarter touches any of the circles, she gets two points. The person with the highest score wins. Each person gets seven tries.

Hand the quarter to your friend, and let her try seven times.

This is really not a game. When you put the quarter on the paper and drew around it with the pencil, lead got all over the edge of the quarter. When your friend tries to roll it down her nose from her forehead, she will make black lines all over her face. When she gets enough lines, pick up the quarter and tell her to look in the mirror. Be prepared to run.

The Last Straw

You will need a straight or safety pin for this little prank.

The next time you are with your friend in a restaurant, bring your pin along. Tell your friend that you will get the straws for the drinks. Take your friend's straw and use the pin to push a hole through the straw. Make two small holes on each end of the straw about an inch from the ends. (Make the holes through the paper wrapper. This way they will not be seen.)

Regardless of which end of the straw your friend puts into the drink this trick will work. The small hole will allow air into the straw when he begins to suck. The drink will remain in the glass; he will get nothing but air.

Potfor

Turn to your friend and say, "Hey, look over there. There goes a Potfor!"

"What's a Potfor?" he will ask.

"To cook in, silly," you reply.

HELLO... MY NaME is POTFOR

Updock

Turn to your friend and say, "You look like you have updock on the seat of your pants."

"What's updock?"

"I don't know. What's up with you?"

Warning

Take a small piece of paper and fold it in half. On the outside write:

WARNING!
DO NOT OPEN OR YOU WILL INSTANTLY
SEE SPOTS BEFORE YOUR EYES

On the inside of the paper write:

SPOTS BEFORE YOUR EYES

Now set the card down where someone will find it. Hide close by so you can see his or her reaction.

Did You Hear?

"Did you hear the joke about the jump rope?"
"No."
"Skip it."

"Did you hear the joke about the hospital?"
"No."
"It will make you sick."

"Did you hear the joke about the ceiling?"
"No."
"Oh, it's probably over your head."

"Did you hear the joke about the peanut butter?"
"No."
"I'd better not tell you, you'd just spread it around."

"Did you hear the joke about the loaf of bread?"
"No."
"It's too crumby to tell."

"Did you hear the joke about the husband and wife who had an argument on their water bed?"
"No."
"They drifted apart."

Crazy Stairs

Study the staircase below. Do the stairs start on the ground level and go up to the right or do the stairs hang from the ceiling on the left?

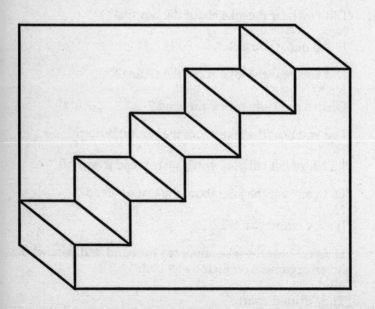

Super Cool Jokes & Games for Kids

Word Puzzles #2

See if you can identify these word puzzles.

DEATH / LIFE	L Y I N G J O B	MIND / MATTER
ECNALG	TOLD TALES TOLD	YOU J U S T ME
-ATTITUDE	HE'S/HIMSELF	E R C T O N U

Crazy Pictures #2

See if you can identify the pictures below . . .

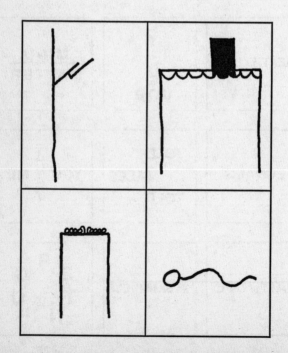

Match This #1

See if you can match these familiar sayings.

1. Black as	_____	A.	a rail
2. Red as	_____	B.	death
3. Dumb as	_____	C.	sugar
4. Quick as	_____	D.	a picture
5. Thin as	_____	E.	a bug in a rug
6. Skinny as	_____	F.	a drum
7. Quiet as	_____	G.	a flash
8. Ugly as	_____	H.	glass
9. Pretty as	_____	I.	a beanpole
10. Pale as	_____	J.	a rose
11. White as	_____	K.	coal
12. Sweet as	_____	L.	sin
13. Sour as	_____	M.	pie
14. Happy as	_____	N.	a kitten
15. Smooth as	_____	O.	an ox
16. Snug as	_____	P.	life
17. Innocent as	_____	Q.	rain
18. Fresh as	_____	R.	gold
19. High as	_____	S.	a bone
20. Large as	_____	T.	a daisy
21. Spry as	_____	U.	a mouse
22. Easy as	_____	V.	the sky
23. Dry as	_____	W.	a lamb
24. Good as	_____	X.	vinegar
25. Tight as	_____	Y.	a lark
26. Right as	_____	Z.	snow

Triangle Trouble

In the drawing below, see how many triangles you can find. Count carefully—there may be more than you think!

Flim-Flam

The Exact Word

Tell your friend that you have the ability to read minds. Ask your friend to write down any word on a piece of paper. Tell her to make sure that you can't see the word, and ask her to fold her paper.

Then tell your friend that you can write down that exact word on another piece of paper. She will probably say, "I bet you can't."

Take your paper and write on it. When you are finished, ask your friend to open her piece of paper and show you her word.

Then open your piece of paper and show your friend what you wrote: That exact word.

The Magic Hat

Tell your friend that you have great magical powers. Tell him you can take a piece of candy (a cookie, cracker, or doughnut will also work), put it under a hat, remove the hat, eat the candy, and then put the candy back under the hat. Then say, "I'll bet I can do it." Your friend will probably say, "I'll bet you can't."

Take the piece of candy and place it on the table. Put the hat over the candy. Lift the hat off the candy. Eat the candy. Your friend will be carefully watching all of these actions. Then turn to him and say, "Now for the hard part. I am going to put the candy back under the hat." Say a few magical words, and then put the hat on your head. You have put the candy under the hat!

A Good Turn

For this trick you will need a cup, a coin, and a handkerchief or napkin.

With your friend looking on, put the coin on the table with the head facing down. Then put the cup over the coin. Next, take the napkin and cover the cup. Have your friend place his hand on top of the napkin covering the cup. Tell him, "I'll bet I can turn the coin from tails to heads without picking up the cup."

He will probably say, "No you can't."

Slide your hand under the napkin and grab the cup. Twist the cup slightly each direction. Then look at your friend and say "I'm ready. Let's see if I win."

Your friend will lift the napkin and cup to see what happened. Reach over and turn the coin. Look at him and say, "I win. I didn't lift the cup—you did."

Strong As a Rope

You will need a paper napkin for this trick.
Take the napkin and twist it tightly into a rope.

Ask your friend to take the twisted napkin and, with a steady pull, break it. It is almost impossible to break the twisted napkin.

After he tries for a while, tell him that you bet that you can pull it the same way he was, and it will break. He will probably say, "No way."

While your friend is pulling on the rope napkin, secretly wet your fingers. When you take the twisted rope from your friend, grab it in the middle with your moistened fingers. Roll the napkin back and forth making sure that the moisture from your fingers penetrates to the center of the napkin.

Then grab both ends of the twisted napkin and pull. It should break apart where the water touched the paper. Try this trick a couple of times alone before you show it to your friend so you will know how wet your fingers should be.

An Impossible Task

Get two objects (anything fairly small will do). Let's say that the objects are two bananas.

Tell your friend, "I'm going to place these two objects in front of you. I'll bet that you won't be able to lift either one of them alone."

Your friend will probably say, "I'll bet I can."

Respond by saying, "I'll bet you can't."

Your friend will reach over and pick up one of the bananas. Don't say anything. Your friend will look at you and say, "See, I did it." To which you say, "Did what?"

"I lifted the banana!"

You smile and say, "I said that you can't pick up either one of the bananas alone. You're not alone; I'm right here with you."

Top This

This is a trick that can be done at a restaurant or at the dinner table. Turn a glass upside down and place it on the table. Put a coin on the glass that has been turned over. Take two straws, toothpicks, or knives and give them to your friend.

Say to your friend, "I'll bet that you can't lift the coin off the top of the glass with these two straws."

Your friend will probably reply, "I can, too."

He will begin to work on the project and will most likely succeed in lifting the coin off the glass. "See, I did it," he will say as he smiles at you.

You say, "No, you didn't. I bet that you could not lift the coin off the top of the glass with the two straws. You lifted the coin off the bottom of the glass."

Add by Subtracting

Pull out a piece of paper and a pen. Tell your friends that you can prove that one from four equals five. (The pen is just to fool them.)

"There's no way you can prove that," they'll say.

"I'll bet you that I can do it," you respond.

They will most likely say, "I'll bet you can't."

Pick up the piece of paper and ask your friends how many corners it has. They will tell you four. Then fold one

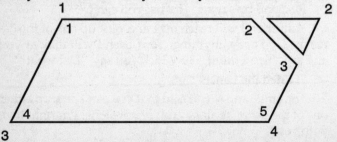

of the corners back forming a triangle. Tear off that corner down the folded line. Then hand the larger piece of paper to your friend and ask them how many corners there are. They will say, "Five."

You have just taken one corner from four corners and have ended up with five corners: $4 - 1 = 5$

Double Twister

Ask your friend to draw two parallel lines on a piece of paper. Then ask her if it is possible for parallel lines to ever cross each other or meet each other. She will say no.

Tell your friend that you know how to draw parallel lines so that they do cross each other and meet each other.

She will probably say, "You're crazy. You can't do it."

You reply, "I'll bet I can."

The drawing will show you how to do it. (The double lines are parallel.)

Ten Thousand

Hand your friend a piece of paper and a pencil and say, "I bet you can't write the number 10,000 without lifting your pencil from the paper. The numbers cannot be linked together by any lines." Let them try several times before you show them how to do it.

First, you fold a piece of paper like the illustration below and write the number 10,000. When you lift the flap only the one and zeros will show.

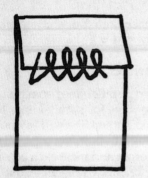 

The Shrinking Quarter

You will need a piece of paper, a dime, a quarter, a pencil, and a pair of scissors for this trick.

Take the dime and place it in the middle of the piece of paper. Make a circle around the dime with the pencil, then cut out the small circle. (You might want to do this a few times, since it's possible that your friend might rip one of the pieces when he tries to do the trick.)

Tell your friend to look at the piece of paper with the hole in it. Ask him to shove the quarter through the dime-size hole in the paper without ripping the paper.

After he gives up, say, "I'll bet I can shove the quarter through the hole without ripping the paper."

He will probably say, "I'll bet you can't."

You say, "I can do it."

Take the paper and fold it in half so that the fold goes right through the middle of the hole. Place the quarter inside the fold, partially sticking out of the hole. Now take the outer edges of the folded paper and carefully bend them up. The hole will expand and the quarter will drop through without ripping the paper. (Make sure not to have a fold in the paper when you hand it to your friend.)

Try this a few times on your own before showing it to someone else.

Double the Hoop

Take a strip of paper about 26 inches long and 2 inches wide. Newspaper works well for this trick. Make a hoop out of the paper. As you bring the two ends together, give one of them a half twist and then tape them together. You have just made a "Möbius Strip."

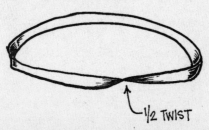

½ TWIST

Take the hoop of paper to a friend and tell him that you can crawl through the hoop without breaking the paper. He will probably say, "I'll bet you can't do it."

After he thinks he has you in a corner, pull out a pair of scissors. Stick one of the points into the paper. Cut lengthwise along the strip of paper until you go completely around. When you finish, the hoop will double its size and you will be able to step through it without tearing it.

Humorous Bible Riddles #3

1. How do we know that the disciples were very cruel to the corn?

2. Why did the rooster refuse to fight on the ark?

3. Why didn't Cain please the Lord with his offering?

4. One of the names of the books of the Bible contains an insect. Which one is it?

5. How many animals could Noah put into the empty ark?

6. Which man in the Bible might have been only 12 inches high?

7. Which book in the Bible is the counting book?

8. What kind of lights did Noah have on the ark?

9. Gideon had 70 sons. How many of them were big men when they were born?

10. Which candle burns longer—the candle hidden under a bushel or the candle set on a hill?

55

Crazy stunts

Jumping Jehoshaphat

Ask your friend if he is very good at jumping. Regardless of what he replies, ask him if he can jump forward from a standing position. Have him demonstrate a small forward jump somewhere in the middle of the room. Next, ask him if he can jump backward from a standing position. Have him demonstrate a small backward jump.

"That's easy," you then say, "because you don't have anything to jump over. I bet you can't jump over this book backward or forward if I place it on the floor." (You can also use a piece of paper or almost any small object.)

Your friend will probably accept the challenge. Ask him if he is ready. When he says, "Yes," you say, "Now, you can't cheat. You can't move the book or touch it once I place it on the floor, OK?" He will agree to the deal.

After he agrees to the rules, walk over to the corner of the room and place the book on the floor. Make sure that it touches both sides of the corner. Then turn to your friend and say, "OK, let's see you jump either forward or backward over the book."

The Vanishing Sugar Packet

This is a good trick to be done at a restaurant when you are with a group of friends. Pick up one of the sugar packets on the table. Look at one of your friends (the victim you have selected) and say, "You know, I have the ability to make this sugar packet vanish before your eyes. I can make it disappear so that you cannot see it, yet everyone else at the table will be able to see it."

Everyone will make different comments.

When they are through, restate, "I can make it disappear so that you cannot see it, yet everyone else at the table will be able to see it. I'll bet I can do it."

Your friend will probably respond, "I'll bet you can't."

Tell everyone that this vanishing trick takes a lot of concentration. You will need everyone's cooperation. Tell them that all eyes need to focus on the sugar packet, and no one is to move a muscle. Restate one more time that you're going to make it vanish from the view of your selected friend, yet everyone else will be able to see it.

Slowly raise the sugar packet off the table. Hold it in front of you so that everyone is watching. If someone talks, ask them to be quiet and concentrate and not move. Say a few magic words and then place the sugar packet on top of the head of the friend that you selected. The packet will vanish from his eyes, but everyone else will be able to see it.

Full of Air

Take a piece of paper and tear off six small pieces about the size of a dime. Place them on your hand, making sure that none of the pieces touch each other.

Turn to your friend and say, "I'll bet you that I can blow these six pieces of paper off my hand with one big blow."

Your friend will most likely respond, "So, that's no big deal. Anyone can do that."

Then you say, "Well, then let's make it a little harder. You choose one of the pieces of paper and put a little X on it. Then put the six pieces of paper on my hand and I will blow off all of the pieces in one breath, except for the one with the X on it. It will remain on my hand."

Your friend will probably say, "I'll bet you can't do it."

You respond, "I bet I can."

Have your friend put the six pieces on your hand in any order he chooses, making sure that none of the pieces touch each other. When that is done, take one of your free fingers and place it on the piece of paper marked with the X. Then blow on the papers really hard. All of the other pieces will fly off except for the one your friend marked. You will have done what you said you were going to do.

Following Orders

Turn to your friend and say, "I have a special feat for you. Please sit in this chair."

After he is in the chair, inform him that you are going to give him an order that he will have to obey.

Tell your friend to get out of the chair. Sometime

he will have to get out of the chair—no matter how much he wants to disobey you.

Sticky Fingers

Tell your friend that you have some invisible "Sticky Glue." Ask your friend to show you her hands. Pretend to put some imaginary glue from an imaginary bottle on her two ring fingers.

Have your friend put her hands together as if she were praying. Then have her lay down, or interlace, her middle fingers while leaving all of the other fingers up in the air. Tell her she can't move her fingers.

Place a quarter or some other coin between her two ring fingers. Tell your friend, "The Sticky Glue really sticks to coins. In fact, the glue is so strong you will not be able to separate your two ring fingers and let the quarter drop."

Your friend will not be able to move her ring fingers until her two middle fingers are raised.

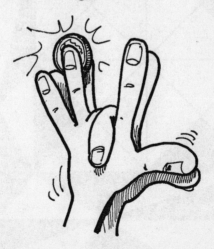

The Triangle Box

Look carefully at the triangle box below. Is the back end of the box larger than the front end of the box?

Humorous Bible Riddles #4

1. Which animal on Noah's ark had the highest level of intelligence?

2. How do we know there were newspaper reporters in New Testament times?

3. The name of one book of the Bible contains an ugly old woman. Which book is it?

4. Which animal on the ark did Noah not trust?

5. Which Bible character was as strong as steel?

6. What man in the Bible is named after a chicken?

7. Where does the Bible suggest that it is okay to be overweight?

8. What Bible character had a name that rang a bell?

9. Which bird on Noah's ark was a thief?

Pick These

The Lumberjack

One day a lumberjack and his assistant went into the forest and chopped down six trees. The assistant said to the lumberjack, "I'll bet you can't cut down six trees and have every one of the fallen trees touching each other at the same time."

"That's easy," said the lumberjack. How did he do it?

Take six toothpicks or pencils and pretend they are the fallen trees. Lay the toothpicks out in a design where each toothpick touches all of the other toothpicks at the same time.

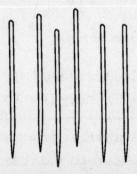

Old MacDonald's Corral

Old MacDonald was a farmer. He had five horse corrals. All of the corrals were the same size. One day Old MacDonald sold one of his horses. He now needed only four horse corrals. But Old MacDonald was a very smart farmer. He realized that if he moved just two of the fences that made five of the corrals, he could make four corrals of the same size. Which two fences did Old MacDonald move?

Below is a diagram of Old MacDonald's five corrals. Take 16 toothpicks and make a corral similar to Old MacDonald's. Can you move two toothpicks (fences) and make four corrals of the same size?

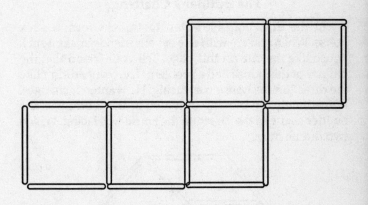

Six to Three

In the drawing below, 17 toothpicks form 6 squares. See if you and a friend can remove any 5 of the toothpicks and leave only 3 of the squares.

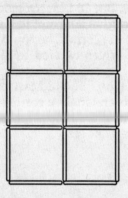

The Builder's Challenge

In the drawing below, ten toothpicks form a stick house. When you are with one of your friends, make a stick house like the one on this page. Tell your friend that the builder of this house had a problem. The owner didn't like the direction the house was facing. He wanted it changed immediately. By moving only two of the toothpicks the builder changed the direction the house was facing. Which two did he move?

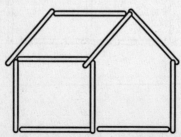

Three to Four

In the drawing below, 12 toothpicks are used to form 3 squares of equal size. By moving only 3 of the toothpicks, see if you can change the 3 squares to 4 squares. This is a simple problem. . . .

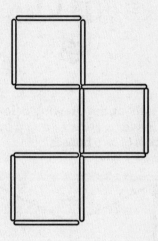

The $\mathscr{B}$ig Ques*t*ion

Look carefully at the drawing below. Do you see a simple room divider . . . or are you up in the sky looking down at the roofs of two houses?

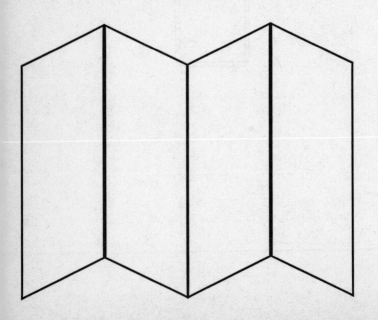

Thought Twisters

1. Are you a good speller? Try this on for size. Make just one word out of the following letters.

   D O J W U N O E T S R

2. The American flag is made up of the colors red, white, and blue. There are 50 stars on the flag. There are 13 stripes, one for each of the original 13 colonies. Are there more red stripes, or are there more white stripes on the flag?

3. How well do you know your sporting events? What game is described: There is no time limit. The defensive team has the ball, and the offensive team can score without touching it.

4. You may have heard of the game Crazy Eights. Try this new game of Crazy Eights. Can you arrange eight 8s so they equal a thousand?

5. Strain your brain and see if you can figure out the only word in the English language that is made up of the following letters:

   SSSSS EEEE N LL P

6. You have used your phone many times. How many times does "O" appear on the button pad?

7. Buffalo Bill rode his horse from Kansas City to San Francisco. He left on Friday and arrived on the very same Friday. How was that possible?

8. What starts with a T, ends with a T, and is full of T?

9. Why is "D" like a bad boy?

10. Why is "A" like noon?

11. What should you keep after you give it to someone?

12. One day you happened to go through your grandfather's attic and found a box filled with his marble collection. The box contained 100 yellow marbles and 100 green marbles. These marbles were all mixed together. How many marbles would you have to pull out of the box to be sure that you would get two marbles of the same color?

13. In the following boxes are three familiar phrases. See if you can find out what is unusual about them.

```
            ┌─────────────────┐
            │  Paris in the   │
            │   the spring    │
            └─────────────────┘
┌─────────────────┐
│   Once in a     │
│   a lifetime    │
└─────────────────┘
            ┌─────────────────┐
            │  Bird in the    │
            │   the hand      │
            └─────────────────┘
```

14. This is a most unusual paragraph. How quickly can you find out what is so unusual about it? It looks so ordinary you'd think nothing was wrong with it. And,

in fact, nothing is wrong with it. It is unusual, though. Why? Study it, think about it, and you may find out. Try to do it without coaching. If you work at it for a bit it will dawn on you. So jump to it and try your skill at figuring it out. Good luck. Don't blow your cool!

15. John Moore liked to brag about his softball team. He told a friend, "Five of our players hit home runs and three of those home runs were hit with the bases loaded. Our team won 11 to 0, and not a single man crossed home plate." How could this be possible?

16. "What has seven legs and gives milk?"
"I don't know."
"A cow."
"A cow?"
"I just gave it three more legs to make the joke harder."

Banana

Turn to your friend and say, "I'll bet I can get you to say banana."

"I bet you can't," she'll reply.

You: "What color is an apple?"

Your friend: "Red or green."

You: "What color is the American Flag?"

Your friend: "Red, white, and blue."

You: "What do cows give?"

Your friend: "Milk."

You: "What do you put into a buttonhole?"

Your friend: "A button."

You: "See, I told you I could make you say baboon."

Your friend: "No, you said banana."

You: "You just said banana!"

Word Puzzles #3

See if you can identify these word puzzles.

SCHOOL	**IS IS IS IS** **IS IS IS** **IS IS** **IS**	**2 PAR** **TON**
IF LAND **IF IF SEA**	T A M H U S W U S T	1T 2T 3T LIFE 4T 5T 6T
MESNACKALS	**CEPS** **CEPS** **CEPS** **CEPS**	**RIFLE** **RIFLE** **RIFLE** **RIFLE** **RIFLE**

71

Fantastic Card Tricks

The Ace of Spades

This is a sure winner of a card trick.

Ask your friend to play a simple game of cards with you. Have him shuffle the deck as much as he'd like. Next, spread the cards face down on the table in front of you. Tell your friend that whoever turns over the ace of spades is the loser of the game. Ask your friend, "Do you want to select first, or would you like me to go first?" Regardless of who starts first, your friend will end up selecting the ace of spades and losing the game.

To start with, the odds are that 50 percent of the time your friend will turn over the ace of spades. This increases your odds to be the winner. But, just to ensure that you do not lose, there is a little secret. Each time you begin to pick up a card, casually lift up the corner of the card and catch a glimpse of what the card is before you turn it over. If it is not the ace of spades, keep turning the card over all in one motion. This way your friend won't suspect what you are doing.

What happens if you note that the card you are about to turn over is the ace of spades? As you lift up the corner of the card and note that it is the ace of spades, do not turn it over. Be sure that your friend sees you looking at the card. Now, set the card aside and pick up another card. Turn it over. Your friend will accuse you of cheating. Ignore his comments. He will then reach over to see what card you laid aside. He will turn it over and discover the ace of spades. He will say, "See—you lost. You had the ace of spades."

You simply smile and ask, "Who turned over the ace of spades? Remember, at the beginning of the game I said whoever *turns over* the ace of spades is the loser."

Follow the Leader

This trick will amaze and fool your friends. You will need two decks of cards. Make sure that both of them are full decks of 52 cards.

Set both decks of cards on the table in front of your friend. Ask her to choose one of the decks and pick it up. Then say, "We are going to play follow the leader. You do what I do. First, I will shuffle my deck of cards, then you shuffle your deck of cards." After doing that, cut your deck a couple of times and have your friend do the same thing. Secretly note what card is at the bottom of your deck.

Next, place your deck on the table. Have your friend place her deck on the table, too. Exchange decks. Then cut your new deck into three equal piles, going from the left to the right. Have your friend copy what you just did.

Take a card off the middle stack and look at it. (Don't memorize it, it's just for show.) Have your friend do the same thing. But have her memorize the card. If there are others present, your friend can show the selected card to them. Then both of you will put the selected cards back on the middle stacks. Next, reach over and put your friend's cards into one pile covering the selected card. Have your friend do the same thing with your cards.

Give your stack to your friend, and you take her stack from her. Cut your deck a couple of times. Have your friend do the same thing to her deck. Then say, "Now look through the deck of cards you're holding in your hand and see if you can find the card you selected. I will do the same thing."

Once she has found her selected card, you place your card face down on the table and have her do the same thing. Then say, "On the count of three turn over your card, and I will turn over mine. One, two, three." There will be a shocked look on your friend's face.

Then say, "Isn't that amazing? We both selected the same card. Do you know that the odds are 2,700 to 1 that that could ever happen?"

They will want to know how you did the trick, but don't tell them. Just go on and do another trick.

The secret to this trick is very simple. When you exchange cards the first time with your friend, you memorized the bottom card of your deck. Remember to have your friend cut the cards into three stacks from left to right. Note the pile that contains the bottom card you memorized.

After your friend has looked at the selected card in her middle stack and replaced it—*you* reach over and put the three stacks into one pile in front of her. Be sure that when you do this, you place the stack with the bottom card that you memorized on top of her middle stack. In this way, your memorized card is on top of her selected card. (Of course, she doesn't know what you are doing.)

Hand the deck in front of you to your friend. She will hand her deck to you. You now have the deck containing her selected card and your memorized card on top of it. Have your friend cut her deck a couple of times. You do the same thing, making sure to cut the cards far enough from the middle to not disturb your memorized card on top of her selected card.

Have your friend look through her deck to find the card she selected. You do the same thing. Only *you* are looking for your memorized card. When you find it, your friend's selected card will be right in front of your card. Now have your friend put her selected card face-down on the table. You do the same thing—picking out her selected card. At the count of three, you both will turn over the same cards.

That is when you say, "Isn't that amazing? We both selected the same card!"

Eyes in the Back of Your Head

This card trick is guaranteed to boggle the minds of your friends.

Have one friend take a deck of cards and shuffle it as many times as he'd like. He can also cut the deck as many times as he'd like. When he thinks the deck is mixed up enough, have him deal 10 cards, face down, in a stack on the table.

Instruct him to pick up the stack of 10 cards and fan them so he is looking at the faces, and you only see the back of the cards. Have your friend mentally select one of the 10 cards and memorize it. If others are present, they can point to the card they selected. Also, have them remember its position from the right. (For example, they may have selected a seven of hearts that is located four cards in from the right.)

Have your friend square up the stack of cards and hand them to you. Take the deck of cards and put them behind your back. Tell your friend that you do much better in figuring out card tricks by putting cards behind your back. Tell him that you have "eyes in the back of your head."

While you are talking about eyes in the back of your head, take three cards from the bottom of the stack and put them on the top of the stack. When that is done bring the stack back out in front of you.

Hand the stack of cards to your friend. Ask him how many cards from the right his memorized card was. Have him take that same amount of cards from the bottom of the stack and move them one at a time from the bottom to the top.

Next, have your friend hand you the top card and put the next card on the bottom of the stack without looking at it. Then repeat that process. Keep doing the same thing until only one card remains. When you turn that card over, it will be the memorized card that your friend selected. He will boggle his mind trying to figure it out.

You can have him deal out another stack of 10 cards and repeat the card trick a second time. (I suggest that you stop after the second time and proceed to another card trick. This will keep him guessing.)

Marvelous Magic

This is another marvelous magic trick that works it-self. Have your friend shuffle a deck of cards until she is satisfied they are mixed up. When she is finished, have her deal three cards, side by side, on the table. Have her continue to deal out cards on those three cards until there are five cards in each of the three stacks.

Have her pick up any one of the stacks. Ask her to select any card in that stack and memorize it. She can show that card to others who might be present. When they have the selected card memorized, have your friend return the card to the deck and shuffle that stack of cards as much as she would like. Then have your friend place that stack on top of one of the two remaining stacks on the table. When that is accomplished, have her place the remaining stack on top of her stack.

Next, have your friend deal out five cards, side by side, on the table, then continue to deal out the remaining cards on top of the cards on the table until there are three cards in each stack. Have your friend turn over all five of the stacks and spread the cards a little so you can see all three cards in each of the stacks. Have your friend point to the stack that has her selected card.

The card in the middle will be your friend's selected card. Quickly memorize that card. Now, have your friend put all the cards together and shuffle them up as much as she'd like. (You already know which card she selected.) When she is satisfied, have her spread out all the cards, face up, on the table. Begin to move the cards around a little. This is just for effect. Pick up five cards from all of those on the table. One of the five cards will be your friend's selected card. Say to your friend, "I think that your card is one of these five cards." Begin to eliminate the cards one by one until there are only two cards left on the table. Then say, "I think that it has to be one of these two cards." Pick up the card that is *not* the selected card. As you do, say, "This is [pause for effect] not it." Quickly put that card down, and pick up the card your friend selected. She will be floored with your great ability.

Same 'O / Same 'O

This card trick will wow your friends every time. Have your friend deal two stacks of cards on the top of a table. Each stack should have 10 cards in it.

Have your friend turn one of the stacks face up. Next, have him shuffle the two stacks of cards together. Have him shuffle as often as he likes and cut the deck as often as he likes. There will be a mixture of 20 cards with some facing up and some facing down.

Have your friend hand you the mixed-up deck. Put the deck behind your back and quickly count 10 cards off the top of the deck into your right hand. Turn the stack of 10 remaining cards over in your left hand. Bring both hands back in front of you and place the two stacks on the table in front of your friend.

Now, for the clincher, tell your friend that there are the same amount of face-up cards in each of the two stacks. Let him count out the number of face-up cards in each stack. When he counts out the same amount, he will be dumbfounded.

Fingerprints

You will have a good laugh with this card trick. All you need is a deck of cards and a regular drinking glass. Have your friend shuffle a deck of cards until he is satisfied that they are mixed up. You take the deck and fan the cards. Allow your friend to select any card and show it to others who might be present.

Turn your back to your friend and say, "I will turn away so I can't see the card you selected." While he is looking at the card, you sneak a quick glance at the bottom card in your left hand. Memorize that card—it will become your key card. When you turn around, have your friend place his selected card on top of the stack in your right hand. Now place the cards in your left hand on top of the cards in your right hand. Your key card is on top of your friend's selected card.

Turn the deck face up. Tell your friend that you will attempt to find the card he chose. Look through the deck until you see the card you memorized. The card directly in front of your key card will be the card your friend selected. Quickly memorize that card.

Continue to look through the deck of cards. When you finally get to the end say, "I'm having trouble finding your card." Then place the deck face up on the table and spread the cards out in no particular order. In fact, it will make the trick even more dramatic if you mess the cards up spreading them every which way. It doesn't matter how messed up the cards get, you already know which card your friend selected!

Say to your friend, "I am going to need some help to find your card." Pick up the drinking glass. "I will use this glass to help me find your card. It will act as a magnifying glass. I will be able to look through it and see your fingerprints on the card you selected." Ask to see the fingers of your friend's hands. Take the glass and pretend to look through it at his fingers. Say, "Okay, I think I have them memorized."

Begin to look at all of the cards on the table. You can make various comments as you pretend to peer through the glass. "Well, I can see my fingerprints on most of the cards. Oh, look at that one, someone must have been eating potato chips when she played cards. I can see the grease." You can make up any comments that may get a laugh.

Eventually, you will find your friend's card. "Here is the card you selected. I can see your fingerprints on it." Pick up the card and hand it to your friend. He will be astounded.

Lie Detector Test

This trick is similar to the "Fingerprints" card trick. Have your friend shuffle a deck of cards until he is satisfied that they are mixed up. You then take the deck and fan the cards. Allow your friend to select any card and show it to others who might be present. If no one else is present, have your friend write down on a piece of paper his selected card. (This way he will not be able to deny that you found the correct card.)

Turn your back to your friend and say, "I will turn away so I can't see the card you selected." While he is looking at the card, sneak a quick glance at the bottom card in your hand. Memorize that card. It will become your key card. When you turn around, have your friend place his selected card on top of the stack in your right hand. Now place the cards in your left hand on top of the cards in your right hand. Your key card is on top of your friend's selected card. Now cut the deck a couple of times, making sure not to disturb the area where your key card and your friend's selected card are located. A little practice will help you accomplish this and make it look impressive.

Turn the deck face up and begin to look through the cards. Tell your friend that you are seeing if everything is in order. Look through the deck until you see the card you memorized. The card directly in front of your key card will be the card your friend selected. Quickly memorize that card.

Now, take the deck of cards and spread them out on the table in a straight line so that you can see all the cards. It looks even more fancy if you spread the cards in an arc like a rainbow.

Pretend to study the cards carefully for a little while. Turn to your friend and say, "I'm having trouble finding your card. I need to use my lie-detector skills to help me."

Ask for the assistance of your friend. Have him make a fist with his right hand and extend his first finger. Tell him that you are going to grab his wrist and move his hand around, using it as a pointer. Tell your friend that you will direct his finger to various cards. When his finger touches a card, you will ask, "Is this your card?" He can say either yes or no.

Tell your friend that your fingers are very sensitive, and you will be able to tell by your friend's pulse whether he is telling the truth or not. Tell him he can attempt to fool you if he wants . . . but you will be able to identify the card he selected.

Begin to use your friend's finger by placing it on any card. Your friend will say either yes or no. You will inform him if he is lying or telling the truth. Eventually, you will end up at the card he selected. Tell your friend that you can feel his pulse racing because this is the card he selected. Your friend and those in the audience will be stunned by your spectacular ability.

Traveling to the Bottom

This card trick is guaranteed to bring a laugh.

Have someone in the group shuffle a deck of cards and hand them to you. You fan out the cards and let three people each select a card. Then turn to a fourth person and have him select and memorize a card. Have him show it to everyone else in the group. While he is doing this, split the deck in half and sneak a glance at the bottom card in your left hand. Have the fourth person put his selected card on top of the stack in your right hand. Place the cards in your left hand on top of that stack. Your key card is now on top of his selected card.

Look through the cards until you find your key card. Split the deck at this point, putting the top half on the bottom of the deck. The fourth person's card should now be on top of the deck. Cut the deck a couple of times making sure that his selected card stays on the top of the deck.

Now turn to the three people holding cards. Have them place their cards on the floor in front of the fourth person. Make sure the cards on the floor are far enough away from the fourth person that he will have to get out of his chair to select one of the cards on the floor.

Tell the audience that you will change one of the cards on the floor into the card selected by the fourth person. Have the fourth person reach forward to select one of the three cards on the floor. As he rises off his chair, a quick push with your right thumb will slip the top card off the deck and onto the chair where he was sitting.

He will select one of the cards on the floor and sit back down. He will sit down on his selected card. You will probably be able to get the card onto his chair without anyone seeing you. If someone does, catch his or her eye and shake your head. The person will most likely go along with the trick. People like to be "in the know."

Now that the fourth person is sitting in his chair, have him place the card from the floor on his knee. Have him turn the card over to see if it is his card. Of course, he will have to say no.

Say, "Well, let me try again." Place the deck in your hand on his knee and have the fourth person tap it several times. Tell him that his card will go to the bottom. Have him look at the bottom card. He will say it is not the correct card. Ask for one more chance to make the trick work.

Take the deck and hold it on top of the fourth person's head. Tap the deck a couple of times and say, "To the bottom . . . to the bottom." Hand the deck to the fourth person and have him look at the bottom card. Again, he will say it is not his card.

Then say, "I think I might have tapped the deck too hard. I think the card you selected might have gone further down. Please stand up—perhaps you're sitting on it." You will get a big laugh out of the group from the fourth person's surprised look.

Flying Card Fun

In the midst of doing card tricks, the "Flying Card" is a fun feat to demonstrate to your friends. All you need is one playing card and a quarter.

Have your friend balance a card on his finger. Then have him place a quarter on the balanced card. Ask him if he can remove the card without touching the quarter or dropping it. Let him try for a while before you show him how to do it.

The secret lies in a quick flick of your fingers. Once the card and quarter are balanced on your finger, hold your middle finger back with your thumb. Apply pressure and quickly release your thumb. The quick flick of your middle finger will knock the card out from under the quarter. The card will fly through the air and the quarter will be resting on your finger. Practice this trick a few times before you show your friends. You will be surprised at how easy it really is.

Bamboozled

For this card trick you will need a special deck of cards prepared in advance. Take a deck with 52 cards in it. Take out 4 cards with the same number. Let's say that you take out all the threes. Next, count out 12 of the remaining diamond cards. Put 6 of the diamonds on the bottom of the deck, 6 of the diamonds on the top of the deck. You will now have a deck containing 48 cards with 6 diamonds on the top and 6 on the bottom.

Hand the prepared deck to your friend. Have him deal off the top 6 cards, side by side. (They will all be diamonds.) Then have him continue to deal, one card at a time, on the 6 stacks until all the cards are gone. (When finished, there will be 6 stacks with a diamond on the top and one on the bottom. Your friend will not be aware of this.)

Have your friend choose any one of the stacks he would like and select a card out of the middle of the stack. Have him memorize the selected card and place it on top of any stack he desires. Then have him choose any stack he wants, and place it on top of his selected card. With the remaining stacks, he can either place them under the large stack or on top of it until there is just one stack with his card somewhere in-between. (In reality, you now know that his selected card is between 2 diamond cards. It will be the only card between diamonds.)

Have your friend pick up the deck and begin to put the cards, face up, one at a time on the table. They can be placed in random spots on the table. As your friend is placing the cards on the table, you will be watching for a diamond, followed by some card, followed by a diamond. You will have to concentrate so that you will not miss that card. When the selected card is placed on the table do not say anything. Let your friend put all the cards on the table.

After all the cards have been placed on the table, rummage through them. Eventually, you will find the selected card. Pick it up and show it to your friend. He will not believe his eyes. This is a stupendous stunner.

Mr. Know-It-All

Mr. Know-It-All is a great ending for card tricks at a party. For this show-stopper, you will need an accomplice. Your accomplice is called "Mr. Know-It-All."

Tell your audience or group that you have a friend named Mr. Know-It-All. He is so smart that the group can select any card from a deck of cards and he will be able to tell what card we selected. All we have to do is select a card and call Mr. Know-It-All on the telephone.

Of course, no one will believe you. Pull out a deck of cards and let someone shuffle the deck. Have another person select the card. Make sure that everyone knows which card was selected. Go to the phone and dial a number.

You will talk to Mr. Know-It-All for a moment, and then turn the phone over to the person who selected the card. When he picks up the phone, Mr. Know-It-All will give him the right answer and then hang up. The person who selected the card will have a total look of shock on his face because Mr. Know-It-All gave him the right answer.

Your friends will ask to see the trick done a second time. It will work the second time just as well as the first. Only, I suggest you have a different person select the card. It would be best to end the trick after two times. You want to leave the group guessing. Be sure not to tell them how to do it.

The secret lies in a predetermined plan of action between Mr. Know-It-All [your friend] and yourself. The following plan is how the trick works. Let's say the selected card was the six of hearts.

1. You call Mr. Know-It-All.

2. You say, "May I please speak to Mr. Know-It-All."

3. Mr. Know-It-All [your friend] then says slowly ... Spades ... Hearts ... Clubs ... Diamonds.

4. As soon as Mr. Know-It-All mentions the right suit, you say, "Hello, Mr. Know-It-All." (In the example, you would say hello as soon as he said hearts.)

5. Mr. Know-It-All will then slowly count ace, two, three, four, five, and so forth, until you say, "Yes, Mr. Know-It-All, it is Bob." (In the example, you would say yes as soon as he said six.)*

6. Mr. Know-It-All will then repeat the card and suit. "The card is the six of hearts."

7. You say, "Yes (to confirm the right answer), I have someone here who would like you to tell him which card he selected."

8. Hand the phone to the person who selected the card.

9. As soon as he says something to Mr. Know-It-All, Mr. Know-It-All, in a strange, weird voice, will say, "You selected the six of hearts." Then Mr. Know-It-All will hang up the phone.

---

*If someone selects one of the high cards you might begin the conversation by saying, "Hi, Mr. Know-It-All" (instead of "Hello"). Mr. Know-It-All will then count, "Ace, king, queen, jack, and so on." That will help speed up the process.

The Builder's Nightmare

Carefully study the drawing below. If you had 12 sticks, could you construct the Builder's Nightmare?

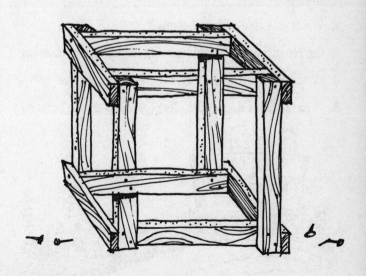

Humorous Bible Riddles #5

1. What is the name of the individual who was perfect in the Bible?

2. What was Eve's formal name?

3. On Noah's ark, why did the dog have so many friends?

4. Who killed a fourth of all the people in the world?

5. What is the name of the sleepiest land in the Bible?

6. When a camel with no hump was born on the ark, what did Noah name it?

7. How long did Samson love Delilah?

8. Where are freeways first mentioned in the Bible?

9. Where does it suggest there may have been buses in the Bible?

Party Tricks

Let's Go for a Spin

This is a fun trick to do at a party. Tell your friends that you have great mental powers. Your brain waves can penetrate through wood. They will probably talk about your blockhead and mention sawdust for brains. Ignore their rude comments. Tell them that you will demonstrate your great mental powers.

Have everyone sit around a wooden table. You sit on the floor under the table. Have your friends take a coin and spin it on top of the table. When it has finally stopped spinning and has fallen down, you will tell them whether it is heads or tails.

Have each person at the table try a spin. Tell them to not let you know who is going to spin the coin to make it harder for you. After you are successful a number of times, you can crawl out from under the table with a big smile on your face. Don't reveal your secret.

The secret is that you have an accomplice in the crowd. Your accomplice will pretend that he is just part of the gang. He will take his turn at spinning like everyone else. The only difference is that when the coin turns up heads your accomplice will slightly raise his right foot. When the coin is tails, he will slightly raise his left foot. If someone looks under the table to see what you are doing, pretend to be looking somewhere else. Also, pretend that you are using great mental concentration. Other people will be moving their feet also. You and your friend should practice a couple of times so no one will see your moves.

Spock's Brain Transfer

This is a good party trick. You will need an accomplice for this trick.

You and your accomplice will tell your friends that you have both developed the ability to transfer brain waves with your hands.

Then you leave the room, and your accomplice will ask the group to come up with a three-digit number. Then he will call you back into the room. Walk over to your accomplice and stand facing him. Neither of you say a word. Place your hands on each side of his face with your fingers touching his temples and the palms of your hands coming down by his jaw. Your palms shouldn't touch your accomplice's jaw.

Look at each other as if in deep concentration. After a few moments, take your hands down. Turn to the group and announce the number they have chosen. Leave the room and do the trick again. It would be wise not to do the trick more than four or five times or your friends might figure out your secret.

The secret is for your accomplice to tighten his jaw muscles and with each tightening count out the first number . . . pause . . . count out the second number . . . pause . . . and then count out the third number.

By placing your fingers on his temples, you can feel the number of counts. By covering his jaws with your palms, you hide the movement of his jaw muscles. Practice a few times before you perform for a group.

A Hole in One

This is a great trick that will impress everyone. You will need two 8½×11-inch pieces of paper (regular notebook paper) and a pair of scissors.

Ask your friend to take one of the sheets of paper and cut the largest hole she can out of her piece of paper.

After she cuts her hole have her try to step through the hole with her entire body. Then take the other piece of paper and say, "I'll bet you I can cut a hole in this piece of paper large enough that I can step through it with my whole body. In fact, if I do it right, the hole will be big enough for both of us to pass through at the same time."

Your friend will probably say, "There is no way you can do that. It's impossible."

You simply smile and say, "I'll bet I can. You just watch."

Take your piece of paper and fold it in half. On the folded side, come in about ½ inch and make a cut that comes to within a ½ inch of the edge of the paper. Then go to the opposite side and do the same thing. Keep doing this until you have made alternate zigzag cuts in all of the paper.

When you have finished with the zigzag cuts, turn the paper to the folded side. Be sure to not cut either end. Start cutting after the first slit, and continue along the crease. Stop just before the end. Now open the paper, being careful not to tear it apart. When you open it up you will find that it forms a hole large enough for you to step through. If you have enough cuts in it, both you and your friend will be able to step through it at the same time. Be sure to practice this trick alone before you try it with a friend.

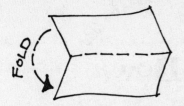

CUT FROM
FOLDED SIDE

MAKE CUTS ON THE
BOTTOM SIDE

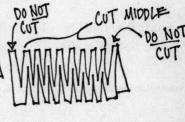

DO NOT
CUT

CUT MIDDLE

DO NOT
CUT

CAREFULLY SEPARATE!

STEP THROUGH
THE HOLE

Up or Down

Study the letter "F" below. Is it sinking into the ground or rising above the ground?

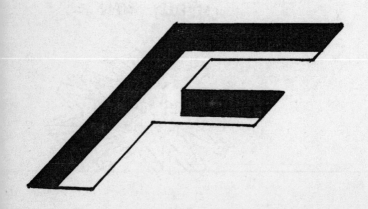

Tricky Fun

X-Ray Vision

Hand your friend four dice. Have him stack the dice on top of each other, noting the total number of the spots on the dice that are hidden from view. There will be a total of seven sides that will not be able to be seen.

Tell your friend that you have wonderful x-ray vision just like Superman. You can look at the top number of the stack of dice and see down through the stack with your x-ray vision. You can count the number of spots hidden from view.

After you give the correct answer, tell your friend, "That was too easy. This time mix up the number of spots so that it will be harder for me." After your friend is done, give the correct answer again. He will be mystified.

The secret is not very difficult. No matter how the dice are stacked, the total number of spots for eight sides will always be 28. Simply subtract the top number of spots from 28. What remains will be the total of the number of the hidden spots.

Spoon Hanging

If you are waiting at a restaurant for your food and are a little bored, you can try "spoon hanging." You can hang the spoon off your nose, your cheekbone, or your chin.

All you have to do is make sure the spoon is warm. You can warm it up by holding it, sticking it in a cup of coffee, or breathing on it until it fogs up.

Hold the handle of your spoon and tip your head slightly back and hang your spoon. Slowly bring your head back, and you will have a spoon hanging on your nose (or cheek or chin).

Magic Knife

Hand your friend five table knives and say, "I'll bet you can't lift four of these table knives by using only the fifth knife. You can choose any one of the knives to be used as the lifting knife."

Let your friend try for a while before you show him how to do the trick. The drawing below shows you how to do it.

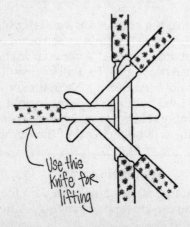

Use this knife for lifting

Imaginary Glue

Take two paperback books about ¾ inch thick. Open both books to the middle, and stick them inside each other. Then have your friend grab them by the bindings and (with a straight pull) pull them apart.

Then tell your friend that you are going to put imaginary glue on the pages—and he will not be able to pull the same two books apart.

Next, take the two paperback books and interlace the pages as if you were shuffling a deck of cards. Fan the pages of book #1 into the pages of book #2. As you are shuffling the pages together, say, "Glue . . . glue . . . glue . . . glue . . . glue." When you have fanned and interlaced the pages of both books together, hand them to your friend.

Ask your friend to grab the bindings in the middle as he did before. Tell him to pull the two books apart with a straight pull. Remind him that he won't be able to do it because of the imaginary glue.

He will not be able to pull the books apart. (The friction on the pages is too great.)

97

I Know the Answer

Give your friend a piece of paper and a pencil. Tell her to choose any number between 1 and 9 and write it on the paper. Have her double the number. Then have her add 12 to the answer. Now have your friend divide the total by 2. When she has finished, have her subtract the number she first wrote down from her last answer.

Then say, "Let me concentrate. The number you ended up with is . . . 6."

She will be astonished at your brilliance. Little does she know that the answer will always be 6.

Turn Over in the Grave

Take a dollar bill and show it to your friend. Make sure that George Washington is facing your friend with his head up. Now, fold the dollar bill in half the long way. Fold George's head down toward your friend.

When the bill is folded in half, fold it in half (sideways) one more time. As you are folding the bill talk to your friend about the economy. Tell her that the father of our country would not be happy with the value of a dollar bill today. (At this point, you should be through folding the bill.)

Begin unfolding the bill the opposite direction. As you do say, "I think that if George Washington knew about our national debt, he'd turn over in his grave." At this point, open up the dollar bill and your friend will find George has turned over (in his grave)!

Floating Metal

Inform your friend that you can make metal float on water. Tell him it won't be an aluminum boat. It will be solid metal.

He will probably say, "That's impossible."

Respond by saying, "Nothing is impossible if you are as smart as I am."

He will most likely groan and say, "Let's see you do it."

Take a pan and pour fresh water into it. Put a small needle on the tines of a fork and slowly lower it into the water. The surface tension of the water will allow the needle to float. Practice this trick a couple of times to see how slowly the needle needs to be put into the water.

The Rule of the Game

You'll need a 12-inch ruler for this trick.

Have your friend hold out one finger on each hand in front of him. Place the ruler on his fingers with his fingers on the 1-inch and 11-inch marks. Have him slowly bring his fingers together. His fingers will meet in the middle—they cannot meet anywhere else.

Next, tell your friend, "I'll bet that you can't slide your fingers back to where they were under the 1-inch and 11-inch marks." Try as he will, he will not be able to do it. One finger will remain in the middle, while the other one moves.

Autographed Fruit

This trick requires that you live in an area that grows fruit and that you have a lot of patience. Let's say you live in an area where they grow red apples. When the apples are green and haven't yet turned red, you will need to start your trick.

Take some masking tape (or any dark tape), and carefully cut out your first name. Go to the tree with green apples and put your "tape name"

99

on the green apple. Then let the sun do the rest. When the apple finally turns red, peel off your "tape name." Where the tape was, the apple will be a different color. You can do this to several apples. You can also put the names of the members of your family on the apples. This trick works on almost any fruit.

When you finally get your apples with names on them, show them to your friends. Tell your friends, "We have a very special apple tree in our garden. We take extra-special care of it. In fact, the tree loves us so much that it produces fruit with our names on them."

When your friends say no way, pull out the apples and show them. If you are in school, you can also put the name of your teacher on some of them. That would really impress him or her.

The Magic Moving Box

Study the drawing below. Look carefully at the box in the center. Is the small box in the center close to you or far away from you?

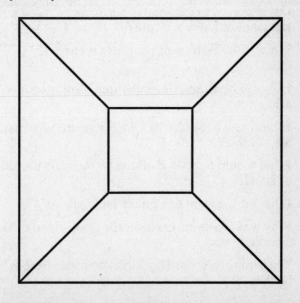

Humorous Bible Riddles #6

1. What did Noah call the cat that fell into a pickle barrel on the ark?

2. How old were the goats when Adam named them in the Garden of Eden?

3. David played a dishonest musical instrument. What was it called?

4. Which Old Testament prophets were blind?

5. How did Noah keep the milk from turning sour on the ark?

6. How many books in the Old Testament were named after Esther?

7. What would happen if all the women left the nation of Israel?

8. Why did the giant fish finally let Jonah go?

9. Why was Moses buried in a valley in the land of Moab near Bethpeor?

10. The name of a book of the Bible contains a fruit. Which book is it?

The Eye Twister

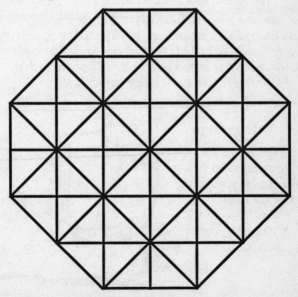

In the drawing below, how many squares and triangles are formed by the lines? Remember—there will be different sizes of squares and different sizes of triangles within the drawing.

Pranks

Too Many T's

Tell your friend that you have a tongue-twister that you would like him to try. The tongue twister is:

Tim the thin twin tinsmith threw teapots.

After he tries the tongue-twister a few times, ask him how many "T's" are in that. Tell him that you will repeat it very slowly so he can concentrate. After you say it again slowly, ask your friend how many "T's" are in that.

Your friend will most likely say, "Nine."

"No," you say, "there are only two 'T's' in 'that.' "

Refrigerator

When you are over at your friend's house ask him, "Is your refrigerator running?"

"Yes."

"Well, you better go catch it."

Television

Turn to your friend and ask, "Did you have your television set on yesterday?"

"Yes."

"How did it fit?"

Owah

Tell your friend that you have just heard about three magical words that will make him very smart. He will ask you what they are. Repeat the following words slowly for him.

OWAH   TAGOO   SIAM

Ask your friend to slowly repeat them. After he is finished, ask him if he feels any smarter. He will probably say no.

Tell your friend it only works if he says them three times very fast. When he does, it will sound like:

Oh what a goose I am.

He has become smart enough to find out that he is a goose!

Frozen Water

Ask your friend, "If frozen water equals iced water, what does frozen ink equal?"

He will probably say, "Iced ink."

To which you say, "You sure do!"

Flip-Flop Word

Ask your friend to write a word that will look the same upside down and right-side up. The word must be written in block letters. You can give him the hint that the word has four letters in it. The flip-flop word is: NOON.

A Sticky Problem

Take a coin and some very strong glue. Glue the coin to the ground in a very busy area. After you put the coin down stand with your foot on it for awhile. (You want to wait for the glue to dry.)

When the glue is dry, step back and have fun watching people try to pick up the coin that is stuck to the ground.

Slap on the Back

This prank is as old as the hills but is still fun. Take a piece of paper about three inches by three inches. Write a note on it and attach a piece of scotch tape or masking tape to it. Walk up behind your friend and give him a pat on the back, and ask him how he is doing. This will attach the note to his back. Because of the pat on the back, he will not know the note is there.

You can put different messages on the note, such as:

Please kiss me

I'm lonely, please say "Hi, Bob"

I'm lost, please help me

Rembrandt

Ask your friend, "Did you know that I am a fantastic painter? I am a great artist." After all his rude remarks, say, "I'll bet you that I can draw a perfect picture of you."

He will probably say, "Okay, let's see it."

Have your friend sit down. Get a piece of paper and a pen or pencil. Pretend that you are drawing his face. Every now and then, look up and continue to pretend that you are drawing. When you are close to finishing your imaginary picture, draw the letter "U."

Turn to your friend and say, "I have drawn a perfect portrait of 'U.' " Then show him your drawing.

The Power of Ten

Take a piece of notebook paper and turn to your friend, saying, "I'll bet you that you can't take this piece of paper and fold it in half 10 times."

Hand it to her and let her try. It is impossible to do.

Button, Button, Who's Got the Button?

Go up to a friend that has a coat with buttons on it. Say, "I'll bet you that I can button up my coat faster than you can. Want to try?"

When she accepts the challenge, say, "All right, get ready, go." She will begin by doing the top button and then go down her coat. You do just the opposite—start at the bottom button and work your way up. Let your friend finish before you do.

She will probably say, "I won!"

Finish buttoning your coat so that she can see you buttoning the last two buttons at the top. Then say, "No, I won. I said that I could button *up* my coat faster than you. You buttoned your coat down; I buttoned my coat up."

Ten Thousand

Turn to your friend and say, "I know you are pretty good with math. Let me give you a little quiz." They may not want to but continue, anyway.

"Come on and try. What comes after 9?"

"Ten."

"Great, I knew you could do it. Okay, what comes after 99?"

"One hundred."

"That's tremendous. What comes after 999?"

"One thousand."

"You're fantastic. What comes after 9,099?"

Most of the time people answer with 10,000. You respond, "Actually, the answer is 9,100. I asked you what came after 9,099."

Rattlesnake Eggs

You will have a lot of laughs with this special prank. It requires some preparation. You will need a paper clip, a rubber band, a small, light-weight washer, a pair of pliers, and an envelope.

On the outside of the envelope write:

BE CAREFUL . . . RATTLESNAKE EGGS!

Take the paper clip and straighten it out. Bend it with the pliers like the drawing below. Next, take the washer and put one end of the rubber band through the hole. Take the long end of the rubber band and loop it through the end that went through the hole in the washer. This will

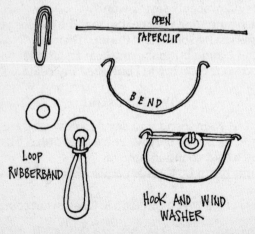

lock the washer to the rubber band. Stretch the rubber band so that it hooks into the slots of the paper clip with the washer in the center.

Now, twist the washer around the rubber band. You are beginning to wind it up. Wind it until the edges of the paper clip start to bend inward a little. Hold the washer and paper clip so it doesn't unwind. Carefully slip the paper clip, rubber band, and washer into the center of the envelope marked RATTLESNAKE EGGS. *Be sure the wire end goes in first.* Carefully close the envelope.

To test your Rattlesnake Eggs, open the envelope. As the envelope opens, the washer will unwind, slapping it against the paper. It will sound like there is something alive in the envelope.

Rewind your washer and prepare your envelope. Set it around for someone to find . . . and watch the fun as he or she picks it up. When the envelope is opened, the noise will probably make your "victim" scream and toss the envelope. This is almost a foolproof laugh-getter.

It might be good to make several envelopes with Rattlesnake Eggs. This way, you can send one to your friend through the mail. Be sure to place the "eggs" in a smaller envelope, then put it into a larger envelope if you are going to mail it. This will keep the "eggs" from unwinding before it gets there. Imagine the shock your friend will have when he or she opens your envelope of Rattlesnake Eggs!

Triangle Time

See if you can guess how many triangles are in the puzzle below.

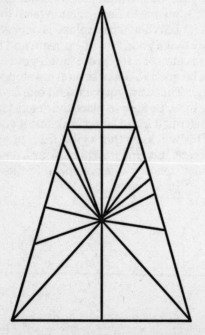

Word Puzzles #4

See if you can identify these word puzzles.

patrol		
iiii / o o	SYMPHON	

		MEN MEN
EVIL **EVIL**	**TIDE**	MEN MEN MEN MEN MEN MAN MEN MEN

| ~~SNOW~~ | VIOLETS
VIOLETS
VIOLETS
VIOLETS
VIOLETS
VIOLETS | 13   4
GOOD
2   46   78
39   5
22 |

111

Wild Stunts

Easy Money

Have your friend stand against a wall. His head, back, bottom, and heels should be touching the wall. Place a dollar on the floor in front of him.

Tell your friend he can have the dollar on the floor if he can pick it up with either hand. The only rule is that he cannot move his heels.

He will try and fail. It is impossible to do.

When he finally gives up, say, "You tried hard but didn't make it. I'll give you a second chance."

Ask him not to move from the spot where he is standing. His head, back, bottom, and heels should still be touching the wall. Tell him that you will give him the dollar if he jumps up in the air from that position.

You have nothing to fear—you will not lose your dollar.

Breakout

Ask your friend if he has ever played "Breakout."

He will probably say, "No. How do you play it?"

You say, "Let's pretend that I am the sheriff in a western town. You are the bad guy, and I am going to lock you up in handcuffs. If you can escape by leaving the room, without unlocking the handcuffs, I will give you a dollar. We won't use real handcuffs. You can just hold your hands together. The only rule is that once I lock the 'handcuffs' you can't let go."

When your friend agrees to the rules, take him over to a piano or a very heavy table. Put his arms around the leg of the piano and "lock" his hands together.

The only way for your friend to leave the room without unlocking his hands is to pick up the piano or table.

Creep Around the Chair

You will need a strong wooden or metal chair for this stunt.

Tie a handkerchief loosely around the back right leg of the chair. Next, sit down in the chair, keeping your feet off the floor.

Swing your legs to the right so they hang over the right side of the chair. Roll onto your right side and slowly creep around the back of the chair. Try to untie the handkerchief on the back right leg of the chair with your teeth.

Next, slip back into a sitting position in the chair with the handkerchief in your teeth—and do the entire stunt without touching the floor.

You will be a real champ if you can go completely around the chair!

The Karate Straw

Hand your friend a potato and a plastic straw. Ask her to pick up the potato using only the straw. She may not wrap the straw around the potato.

After she struggles for a while, show her how to do it.

Pick up the straw, placing your thumb over one end. Place the potato on the table in front of you. With a quick downward motion drive the straw into the potato. As long as you hold your thumb on one end, air will stay in the straw. The air inside the straw makes it stronger when it hits the potato. It also helps keep the straw from bending. Once the straw has been driven into the potato, it will be easy to pick it up with a slow, gentle, upward motion.

Practice this trick a few times before you show it to your friends. It takes a couple of times before you see how fast and hard to drive the straw into the potato.

Parallel Puzzle

Study the drawing below. Are the horizontal lines parallel to each other or do they slant?

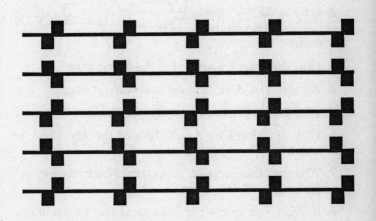

Humorous Bible Riddles #7

1. What does the wall of Jerusalem have that the Israelites didn't put there?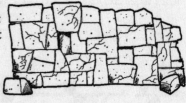

2. Why is the "W" the nastiest letter in the Bible?

3. How did Joseph learn to tell the naked truth?

4. What food did Samson eat to become strong?

5. Why did the tower of Babel stand in the land of Shinar?

6. Why did Moses have to be hidden quickly when he was a baby?

7. What two things could Samson the Nazarite never eat for breakfast?

8. If Elijah were invited to dinner and was served only a beet, what would he say?

9. If a man crossed the Sea of Galilee twice without bathing, what would he be?

More Flim-Flam

Super Brain

Tell your friend that you have such a "super brain" that you can read his mind. Tell him you will give him an example. Ask your friend to think of 2 numbers from 1 to 9. Have him select either of the 2 numbers without telling you which one he selected. Then have him:

1) Multiply the selected number by 5.

2) Add 7 to that number.

3) Double the above result.

4) Add the other original number.

5) Subtract 14 from the above answer.

Have your friend share the result with you. The answer will be a two-digit number. *Both of the two digits will be the original two numbers your friend selected in the beginning!*

The Frightened Finger

Have your friend put one of his hands flat on a table. Next, ask him to take his middle finger (the longest one) and fold it under his palm. (The knuckle of the middle finger should be flat on the surface of the table while all of the other fingers are extended.)

Now, tell your friend that you have the power to "frighten" one of his fingers. When the chosen finger becomes frightened, it can't be lifted off the table. Then touch his ring finger and say, "This is your frightened finger. You will not be able to lift it off the table."

Keep your finger on the "frightened finger," and have your friend lift his thumb . . . then his index finger (first finger) . . . and his little finger off the table one at a time.

Now, remove your finger from your friend's ring finger. Have your friend try to lift his ring finger off the table. He will not be able to do it!

Quick Hands

Have your friend open the palm of her hand in front of her. Place a coin in the palm of her hand. Hold your hand about 6 inches above her palm with your fingers down.

Tell your friend that she can have the coin, if she can close her hand before you can grab the coin. The only rule is that your friend cannot move her hand or close her hand until you make the first move.

Don't worry, you should be able to grab the coin every time. When your fingers hit the palm of your friend's hand, the coin will jump into your hand.

Going Bananas

Take a small piece of paper and fold it in half. Then open it and write the following words on it in the following order.

BANANA BANANA
SAY   BANANA

CLOWN	BANANA
THIS	BANANA
MADE	BANANA
I	BANANA
TIMES	BANANA
MANY	BANANA
HOW	BANANA
LOOK	BANANA

Now fold the paper back so that the BANANA words are on one side, and the other words are on the back side. Hand the paper to your friend and have him read it—the BANANA side first. Then have him turn it around and read the other words.

Next, open the paper and have him read all the words from the top down. BANANA/BANANA . . . SAY/BANANA . . . CLOWN/BANANA, and so forth until he reaches the bottom.

Finally, have your friend read the right column from the bottom up, BANANA, BANANA, BANANA . . . until he reaches the top. Ask him to read the left column from the bottom up. Now you have really got him.

Blowhard

You will need a soda pop bottle and a napkin for this trick.

Take a piece of the napkin and roll it into a loose ball a little smaller than the opening of the soda pop bottle. Place the piece of rolled paper just inside the neck of the bottle while the bottle is on its side.

Say to your friend, "I'll bet you can't blow this piece of paper into the bottle while it is on its side."

He will take the challenge. Just before he tries, say, "You had better take a deep breath. It's harder than you think."

When your "blowhard" friend tries, he will not succeed. The wind blown into the bottle forces the paper *out* of the bottle instead of in the bottle. Your friend will get a wad of paper in his face.

Air Force

Place a ruler on a table so that about one third of it sticks over the edge. Take a large sheet of paper and place it over the ruler.

Tell your friend, "I'll bet you can't hit the end of the ruler [that sticks over the table] and make the paper fly into the air.

As many times as he tries, he will not be able to do it. The friction created by the paper will make it impossible. The paper will stay with the ruler. Be sure not to hit the ruler too hard—you might break it.

Very Impressive

Give your friend a pencil or pen and a piece of paper. Have her write down any three digit number she wants. Tell her to be sure that you cannot see what she is writing down. Next, have her reverse the numbers and subtract the smaller three-digit number from the larger three-digit number.

Finally, ask your friend what the last digit number to the right is. As soon as she informs you of that number, you will tell what her three-digit answer is. This trick is very impressive and works every time.

Whenever you subtract a three-digit number from its reverse the middle number will always be nine. Your friend has told you what the last digit is. At this point you have the answer to the second and third digits. The last digit and the first digit will always total nine when added together. Since you already know the last digit, subtract it from nine and that will tell you what the first number is. If your friend tells you the last digit is nine, you automatically know the answer is 99.

Examples:

421   Chosen number

<u>124</u>   Reversed number

297

The middle number is always a nine

$2 + 7 = 9$. The answer is 297.

Handcuffed

1. Get two safety pins (large ones work best). (See Diagram 1.)

2. Position your safety pins exactly as shown in Diagram 2. Then close the open one. Your safety pins should look like Diagram 3.

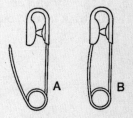

Diagram 1

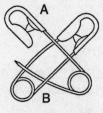

Diagram 2

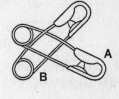

Diagram 3

3. Now, grab the end loop of B with one hand and the head of A in the other.

4. Holding B firmly, quickly jerk A toward you and down, while sliding it toward the B head. This slides A off of B (See Diagram 4.)

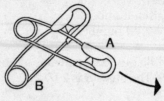

Diagram 4

5. The safety pins are separated but still closed. Although this trick takes a bit of practice, you will really amaze everyone!

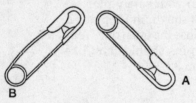

Diagram 5

Math Wizard

Tell your friend that you can read his mind. Tell him that you will give a demonstration of your amazing ability.

1. Ask him to write down a number.

2. Tell him to double that number.

3. Have him multiply the above number by five.

4. Ask him to share the result.

5. Drop off the zero on the end, and what remains will be the number he started with.

Word Puzzles #5

See if you can identify these word puzzles.

Crazy Pictures #3

Can you guess what the pictures below mean?

Mind Warpers

1. How many times can you subtract the number 10 from the number 50?

2. People rarely agree when it comes to politics and religion. What is one thing that all wise people, regardless of their political or religious position, agree upon when it comes to what is between heaven and earth?

3. Moving forward I become very heavy. Moving backward I'm not. What am I?

4. What word starts with is . . . ends with nd . and has la in the middle?

5. Three salesmen checked into a hotel. The clerk charged them $30 for the night ($10 a bed). The following morning, the hotel clerk realized that he had overcharged the men. The room should have only cost $25. He gave the bellhop $5 to give back to the three men. The bellhop decided to keep a $2 tip for himself. He gave the three men $1 each. The men were very happy to get a dollar back. They looked at each other and said, "Great! We only paid $9 each." Nine times 3 equals 27. The bellhop kept $2 for himself. Two dollars plus $27 equals $29. What happened to the other dollar?

6. Ralph is a little strange. He has a large collection of socks. He likes blue socks and red socks. In fact, he has 30 red socks and 30 blue socks. He keeps his socks in a box in his dark closet. Since it is dark and very difficult to see, what is the smallest number of socks he has to remove to get two socks of different colors?

7. A very mean king went to a nearby village. He wanted some more slaves to serve him at his royal palace. He decided that if any family in the village had more than five children he would take them. The cobbler and his wife had ten children. When the king came to take them, the cobbler and his wife begged and begged. Finally the king said, "I see that you have ten pairs of shoes in a box. If you can give each of your children a pair of shoes and still leave one pair out of ten in the box, you can keep your children." The cobbler and his wife began to smile at each other. How did they keep all of their children?

8. A police dog is tied to a rope that is 10 feet long. The dog's food dish is by the house 13 feet away. Without chewing the rope in half, the dog figures out how to get to his food dish. How does he do it?

9. Math can sometimes be very tricky. If you were to take six bananas from ten bananas, and then take three bananas from the six bananas, how many bananas would you have?

10. How many six-cent stamps are in a dozen?

11. What occurs once in every minute . . . twice in every moment . . . yet never in a thousand years?

12. Mr. and Mrs. Cross have five children. Half of them are girls. How can this be.

13. It was a very cold day in Alaska—it was 10 degrees below zero. Upon returning to his cabin, a gold miner discovered that he had only one match left. As he looked around his cabin he saw the fireplace, the kitchen stove, a candle, and a kerosene lamp. What should he light first?

14. How can you physically stand behind your brother while he is standing behind you?

15. Professor Lilley gave a lecture upon his return from a trip to the pyramids of Egypt. He told of discovering a tomb of an ancient Pharaoh that dated back to 115 B.C. In the tomb were large stone trunks filled with coins and jewels. He said that he saw some coins that dated from 115 B.C. to 75 B.C. He also discovered how they embalmed the mummies by reading the writing on the walls of the tomb. All of a sudden a Middle East expert jumped up and said, "Professor Lilley, you are a fake." Why was Professor Lilley challenged?

16. How many cubic feet of dirt are in a hole three feet square by seven feet deep?

17. An explorer found three old sacks. The first sack was labeled "Gold." The second sack was labeled "Silver." The third sack was labeled "Diamonds." Each sack had been labeled incorrectly. How could the

explorer label each sack correctly if he were only allowed to look into one of the sacks?

18. A black cat ran from the sidewalk to the middle of the street. This cat lived in a town where every building was built out of black brick and mortar. None of the street lights or lights in rooms with windows were working due to power failure. A man in a yellow sports car was driving down the street. The fuses in his car had burned out, and his headlights were not working. Yet this man turned his sports car just in time to avoid hitting the black cat. How did the driver see the cat in time?

Tantalizing Triangle

Carefully study the Tantalizing Triangle below. Follow the lines and determine how it was constructed. Get three pieces of wood and see if you can build your own tantalizing triangle.

Match This #2

Find and match the opposite meanings for the numbered words.

1. Impromptu _____   A. Trusting

2. Exonerate _____   B. Praise

3. Expose _____   C. Hideousness

4. Immaculate _____   D. Distort

5. Renovate _____   E. Frankness

6. Rejoice _____   F. Pliable

7. Pulchritude _____   G. Persecute

8. Portray _____   H. Repair

9. Despair _____   I. Planned

10. Rigid _____   J. Unclean

11. Fragile _____   K. Ruin

12. Disparage _____   L. Hope

13. Flattery _____   M. Grieve

14. Skeptical _____   N. Tough

15. Damage _____   O. Conceal

Crazy Pictures #4

Can you guess what the pictures below mean?

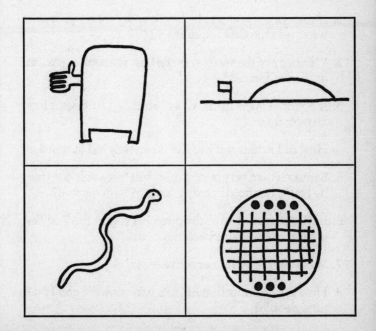

Humorous Bible Riddles #8

1. If someone wanted to be baptized by John the Baptist, what was the first requirement?

2. What day of the week was the best for cooking manna in the wilderness?

3. If a soft answer turns away wrath, what does a hard answer do?

4. How did Adam and Eve feel when they left the garden?

5. Samson was a very strong man, but there was one thing he could not hold for very long. What was that?

6. If Moses would have dropped his rod in the Red Sea, what would it have become?

7. What fur did Adam and Eve wear?

8. How do we know that Elijah's parents were good business people?

9. Jesus and the giant fish that swallowed Jonah have something in common. What is it?

10. What is it that Adam never saw or possessed, yet left two for each of his children?

Math Magic

This is a fabulous trick that will fool almost every one. Ask your friend to select any number from 1 to 63. Tell him not to let you know which number he selected. Have him write the number down on a piece of paper.

Then hand him a copy of the six pieces of paper illustrated below. (You can take this book to a copy machine and copy the six boxes listed below. After they are copied, cut them out so that you have six individual pieces of paper.)

Have your friend look at the six pieces of paper to see if the number he selected is on them. Have him put the paper(s) with his number in one pile and the papers without his number in another pile.

Pick up the paper(s) that include your friend's selected number. Quickly look at each of them and then tell your pal what his selected number was. Have him show you the number he wrote down. He will be blown away by your magnificent mental ability!

The way to find out your friend's number is to add together the numbers listed in the top left-hand corner of the sheets of paper selected by your friend. That total will be the number your friend selected.

1	3	5	7	9	11	13	15
17	19	21	23	25	27	29	31
33	35	37	39	41	41	45	47
49	51	53	55	57	59	61	63

2	3	6	7	10	11	14	15
18	19	22	23	26	27	30	31
34	35	38	39	42	43	46	47
50	51	54	55	58	59	62	63

4	5	6	7	12	13	14	15
20	21	22	23	28	29	30	31
36	37	38	39	44	45	46	47
52	53	54	55	60	61	62	63

8	9	10	11	12	13	14	15
24	25	26	27	28	29	30	31
40	41	42	43	44	45	46	47
56	57	58	59	60	61	62	63

16	17	18	19	20	21	22	23
24	25	26	27	28	29	30	31
48	49	50	51	52	53	54	55
56	57	58	59	60	61	62	63

32	33	34	35	36	37	38	39
40	41	42	43	44	45	46	47
48	49	50	51	52	53	54	55
56	57	58	59	60	61	62	63

Answer Key

Brain-Benders (page 13)

1. Katherine's ring slipped off her finger and fell into an opened can of *dry* coffee.
2. The beautiful parrot was deaf.
3. Nole suggested that the truck driver let some air out of the truck's tires. This would lower the truck enough to squeeze under the underpass. Once the truck passed through, the driver could stop at the service station and put air back in his tires.
4. I'll tell you tomorrow.
5. "What-do-you-think" is not a question. It is the name of the horse.
6. Mr. Anderson solved his problem by turning the square of his new house on an angle (like a diamond). (Remember that doubling the size does not mean twice the length and twice the width. That would increase Mr. Anderson's house square footage by 4 times.)

7. The big game hunter stuck his finger in his ear and asked, "Did you do this?"

8. It would be very easy for the blindfolded man to hit the hat if the hat were hanging on the barrel of the rifle that you handed to him.
9. Unusual.
10. A mirror only reflects what is directly across from it.
11. The month is April. During April, the clocks are set ahead one hour for daylight savings time. On that day there are only 23 hours instead of 24 hours. April will have 29 days and 23 hours in it, making it the second shortest month.
12. North and south are stationary or fixed points. East and west are general directions. East and west would stay the same.
13. "Mispelled" should be "misspelled."
14. No "L" (noel).
15. 10.
16. Only one, then it wouldn't be empty anymore.
17. 20 seconds before 3 P.M. (2.59.40). The box hold only two tennis balls.
18. (5+5)×(5+5)=100.
19. "My feet—from off the floor."
20. Willard and Elmo were two goldfish. The household dog wanted to get a drink of water. He knocked over the bowl and it fell to the floor breaking into pieces. Later the water dried up.
21. C.
22. Because the watchman was supposed to be guarding the bank—not sleeping on the job.
23. 380 feet (there are 19 spaces between the trees).
24. There are 19 letters: T-H-E-E-G-Y-P-T-I-A-N-A-L-P-H-A-B-E-T.
25. 3.
26. C.
27. Because the pilot was flying his plane upside down.
28. He deduced that the coal, the scarf, and the old hat were placed on a snowman. The warm spring had melted the snowman and helped the grass to grow.

A Square Deal (page 20)

There are 14 squares.

Humorous Bible Riddles #1 (page 21)

1. The "fast" days.
2. The letter "a."
3. His second son. He was always a Ham.
4. When Adam and Eve played hide-and-seek with God.

5. He knew a Lot.
6. The Bible.
7. Because they always said neigh.
8. Adam, when God removed one of his ribs (Genesis 2:21).
9. When the children of Israel crossed it.
10. Leeks.

Word Puzzles #1 (page 27)

1. Sandbox.
2. Eggs over easy.
3. Crossroads.
4. Pie in the sky.
5. Reading between the lines.
6. Turning over a new leaf.
7. Long underwear.
8. Bottomless pit.
9. Tricycle.

Crazy Pictures #1 (page 28)

1. A tic-tac-toe game after an earthquake.
2. An elephant with a runny nose.
3. Three elephants on the other side of a fence.
4. The end of the line.

Humorous Bible Riddles #2 (page 34)

1. He knew there was something fishy in it.
2. Because He can take a "rib."
3. Time to get a new chair.
4. His promises.
5. The night—because the day was light.
6. Baby skunks.
7. Vanity (vani-tea).
8. Judges.
9. The mockingbird.
10. Tide.

Word Puzzles #2 (page 43)

1. Life after death.
2. Lying down on the job.
3. Mind over matter.

4. Backward glance.
5. Twice told tales.
6. Just between you and me.
7. Negative attitude.
8. He's beside himself.
9. Counterclockwise.

Crazy Pictures #2 (page 44)

1. A soldier walking behind a building.
2. Abraham Lincoln taking a shower.
3. A fish's view of a diving board.
4. A bird's view of a flagpole.

Match This #1 (page 47)

1. K—Black as coal.
2. J—Red as a rose.
3. O—Dumb as an ox.
4. G—Quick as a flash.
5. A—Thin as a rail.
6. I—Skinny as a beanpole.
7. U—Quiet as a mouse.
8. L—Ugly as sin.
9. D—Pretty as a picture.
10. B—Pale as death.
11. Z—White as snow.
12. C—Sweet as sugar.
13. X—Sour as vinegar.
14. Y—Happy as a lark.
15. H—Smooth as glass.
16. E—Snug as a bug in a rug.
17. W—Innocent as a lamb.
18. T—Fresh as a daisy.
19. V—High as the sky.
20. P—Large as life.
21. N—Spry as a kitten.
22. M—Easy as pie.
23. S—Dry as a bone.
24. R—Good as gold.
25. F—Tight as a drum.
26. Q—Right as rain.

Triangle Trouble (page 46)

There are 38 triangles.

Humorous Bible Riddles #3 (page 55)

1. Because they pulled its ears.
2. Because he was chicken.
3. He wasn't Able.
4. Ti-moth-y.
5. One. After that the ark wouldn't be empty.
6. Nicodemus—because he was a ruler (John 3:1).
7. Numbers.
8. Floodlights.
9. None of them; they were all babies.
10. Neither one; they both burn shorter.

Humorous Bible Riddles #4 (page 61)

1. The giraffe.
2. Because Zacchaeus couldn't see Jesus "for the press" (Luke 19:3).
3. Hag-gai.
4. The cheetah.
5. Iron (Joshua 19:38).
6. Hen (Zechariah 6:14).
7. Leviticus 3:16: "All the fat is the LORD's."
8. Mehetabeel (Ma-hit-a-bell) (Nehemiah 6:10).
9. The robin.

Pick These

The Lumberjack (page 62)

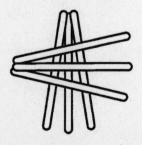

Old MacDonald's Corral *(page 63)*

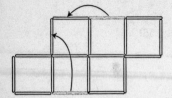

Six to Three *(page 64)*

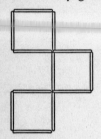

The Builder's Challenge *(page 64)*

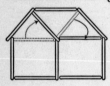

Three to Four *(page 65)*

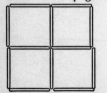

Thought Twisters (page 67)

1. Just one word.
2. There are seven red stripes and six white stripes.
3. Baseball.
4.   8
         8
         8
        88
        <u>888</u>
       1000
5. Sleeplessness.
6. Three times (twice on the operator button).
7. Friday was the name of his horse.
8. A teapot.
9. Because it makes ma mad.
10. Because it is the middle of day.
11. Your word.
12. Three marbles.
13. The three unusual phrases read as follows:

    Paris in *the the* spring

    Once in *a a* lifetime

    Bird in *the the* hand

14. The paragraph leaves out the most common letter in our alphabet—the letter "e."
15. All the players were married men.

Word Puzzles #3 (page 71)

1. High school.
2. Tennis.
3. Not up to par.
4. One if by land; two if by sea.
5. What goes up must come down.
6. Life begins at 40.
7. Snack between meals.
8. Forceps.
9. Repeating rifle.

Humorous Bible Riddles #5 (page 88)

1. Mark—"Mark the perfect man, and behold the upright" (Psalm 37:37).

2. Madam Adam.
3. Because he wagged his tail instead of his tongue.
4. Cain, when he killed Abel (Genesis 4:1-8).
5. The land of Nod (Genesis 4:16).
6. Humphrey.
7. Until she bald him out.
8. Genesis 1:30—"The Lord made every creeping thing" (author's paraphrase).
9. In Proverbs 30:31, where it talks about the greyhound.

Humorous Bible Riddles #6 (page 102)

1. A sourpuss.
2. They were only kids.
3. The lyre.
4. Ezra, Hosea, Joel, Amos, Jonah, Nahum, and Habakkuk. None of them have i's.
5. He left it in the cow.
6. 22—the rest were named before Esther.
7. It would be a stag-nation.
8. It couldn't stomach him.
9. Because he was dead.
10. Phi-lemon.

The Eye Twister (page 103)

There are 38 squares and 124 triangles.

Triangle Time (page 110)

There are 53 triangles.

Word Puzzles #4 (page 111)

1. Circles under eyes.
2. Unfinished symphony.
3. Border patrol.
4. Lesser of two evils.
5. Soapbox.
6. Man among men.
7. Dashing through the snow.
8. Shrinking violets.
9. Good with numbers.

Humorous Bible Riddles #7 (page 116)

1. Cracks.
2. Because it always makes ill will.
3. By exposing the bare facts.
4. Mussels.
5. Because it couldn't sit down.
6. Saving him was a rush job.
7. Lunch and supper.
8. That beet's all.
9. A dirty double-crosser.

Word Puzzles #5 (page 123)

1. Ground swell.
2. Icebox.
3. Long time no see.
4. High class.
5. Downstairs.
6. Split personality.
7. Backpedal.
8. Leaning over.
9. A round of applause.

Crazy Pictures #3 (page 124)

1. Five elephants after the same peanut.
2. A man playing a trombone in a phone booth
3. An outspoken wheel.
4. The early bird caught by a very big worm.

Mind Warpers (page 125)

1. Once. After you subtracted 10 from 50, it would be 40.
2. The word "and."
3. The word "ton."
4. Island.
5. To find the missing dollar, add the $25 received by the hotel clerk to the $3 given to the men. That would total $28. Then add the $2 kept by the bellhop for a tip. You have now found the missing dollar.
6. 31 socks.
7. The cobbler gave each of his nine children a pair of shoes. That left one pair in the box. He then handed his tenth child the box

8. He walks over to the dish. The rope isn't tied to anything except the dog.
9. Six bananas. What you take is what you have.
10. 12.
11. The letter "m."
12. All the Cross children are girls.
13. The match.
14. All you have to do is stand back to back.
15. Professor Lilley was challenged because coins were never dated "B.C."
16. None. There is no dirt in a hole.
17. The explorer selected the sack labeled "Gold." Inside, he found diamonds. That left two sacks labeled "Silver" and "Diamonds." If diamonds were in the gold sack, that left silver and gold. Since all of the sacks were labeled incorrectly he knew the answer. Gold had to be in the silver sack, and silver had to be in the diamond sack.
18. The driver in the yellow sports car had no difficulty missing the black cat because it happened in the middle of the day.

Match This #2 (page 130)

1. I—Planned.
2. G—Persecute.
3. O—Conceal.
4. J—Unclean.
5. K—Ruin.
6. M—Grieve.
7. C—Hideousness.
8. D—Distort.
9. L—Hope.
10. F—Pliable.
11. N—Tough.
12. B—Praise.
13. E—Frankness.
14. A—Trusting.
15. H—Repair.

Crazy Pictures #4 (page 131)

1. A man in a mailbox making a left turn.
2. A fat man in a bathtub smoking a pipe.
3. A worm waiting for the early bird.
4. Neat spaghetti and meatballs.

Humorous Bible Riddles #8 (page 132)

1. He had to go from bad to immerse.
2. Friday.
3. It turns wrath your way.
4. A little put out.
5. His breath.
6. Wet.
7. Bareskin.
8. Because they made a prophet.
9. Jesus had dinner with a sinner, and the giant fish had a sinner for dinner.
10. Parents.

Other Books by Bob Phillips